BLINDSIDE

BLINDSIDE

How to Anticipate Forcing Events and Wild Cards in Global Politics

Francis Fukuyama, *editor*

An *American Interest* Book

BROOKINGS INSTITUTION PRESS
Washington, D.C.

Blindside: How to Anticipate Forcing Events and Wild Cards in Global Politics
may be ordered from:
BROOKINGS INSTITUTION PRESS
c/o HFS, P.O. Box 50370, Baltimore, MD 21211-4370,
Tel.: 800/537-5487; 410/516-6956; Fax: 410/516-6998
Internet: www.brookings.edu

The Library of Congress has cataloged the hardcover edition as follows:
Blindside : how to anticipate forcing events and wild cards in global politics / Francis Fukuyama, editor.
p. cm.
"An American Interest Book."
Summary: "Focuses on developing analytical tools to anticipate and manage low-probability events. Addresses psychological and institutional obstacles preventing planning for low-probability tragedies and allocating necessary resources. Pinpoints failures—institutional and personal—that allowed events to surprise leaders and examines philosophies and methodologies of forecasting. Discusses low-probability, high-impact contingencies in various sectors"—Provided by publisher.
Includes bibliographical references and index.
ISBN-13: 978-0-8157-2990-7 (cloth : alk. paper)
ISBN-10: 0-8157-2990-1 (cloth : alk. paper)
1. Emergency management—United States. 2. International relations. I. Fukuyama, Francis. II. Title.
HV551.3.B57 2007
363.34'7—dc22 2007027757

ISBN-13: 978-0-8157-2991-4 (pbk. : alk. paper)

Digital printing

Printed on acid-free paper

Typeset in Minion

Composition by Peter Lindeman
Arlington, Virginia

Contents

BLINDSIDE

1

The Challenges of Uncertainty: An Introduction

Francis Fukuyama

The collapse of communism, the rapid emergence of China and India as major economic powers, the September 11 attacks, the appearance of relatively new diseases like HIV/AIDS and H5N1 bird flu, Hurricane Katrina—the past decade and a half has demonstrated that nothing is as certain as uncertainty in global politics. As the famous scatological bumper sticker suggests, bad things happen. But there are benign surprises as well, and these, no less than catastrophic events, challenge society's capacity to understand, to adapt, and to lock in good fortune.

Anticipating and dealing with what were thought to have been very low-probability events have clearly become central challenges for policymakers in public and private sectors alike all over the world. This book, sponsored by *The American Interest* magazine, addresses those challenges. The magazine's first annual event, held in Washington, D.C., in May 2006, brought together analysts, practitioners, policymakers, and unconventional thinkers from a variety of backgrounds and disciplines. The magazine assembled those who think about discrete uncertainties and who also have considered the very nature of uncertainty itself. The distinction may seem a minor one, but it is not. Many people, from intelligence analysts to investment bankers to corporate treasurers, are paid to think about discrete futures in their areas of professional responsibility. But far fewer people have ever tried to understand *why* the future is inherently difficult to anticipate, and how to mitigate our blindness to its vicissitudes in a more systematic way than societies and governments have been able to do heretofore.

The task is a complex one. Those who deal professionally with global politics, foreign policy, and national security affairs have particular biases when it comes to thinking about the future. Those biases generate a perceptual incentive structure that throws off their general capacity for accurate prediction. Such analysts, after all, are seldom rewarded for predicting continuity or the sudden emergence of good news, but failure to predict bad news can be a career-ending mistake. No one wants to be in the position of Admiral Husband Kimmel, the commander of the U.S. Pacific Fleet, who was on duty the day of the Japanese attack on Pearl Harbor. Admiral Kimmel's code-breakers had deciphered the Japanese "winds" code, but he, the principal consumer of that intelligence, nonetheless failed to anticipate that the actual blow would land on the Pacific Fleet headquarters. The day that would live in ignominy well described the resting place of Admiral Kimmel's reputation for all time.

By contrast, no one in the U.S. intelligence community was cashiered for failing to predict that the Berlin Wall would come down in November 1989, though fail to predict it they did. This asymmetry in incentives leads the vast majority of those who work on national security issues to resort routinely to worst-case analysis as a means of covering themselves in case bad things happen on or just beyond their watch.

Investment bankers and corporations, in contrast, have much more balanced incentives to think about the future. For them, a failure to anticipate an opportunity can have very costly consequences—indeed, upside potential is often greater than downside, since one can only lose what one owns in an unleveraged situation. Businessmen may even be guilty of laboring under incentive structures that are biased toward excessive optimism.

The bias against optimism in the governmental intelligence world was nowhere more evident than in the estimates made of Iraqi weapons of mass destruction (WMD) before the 2003 Iraq invasion. After the entry of United Nations inspectors into Iraq in the wake of the 1991 Gulf War, the intelligence community found itself in a Husband Kimmel–type situation. Iraq was far closer to a nuclear capability than anyone outside of the Iraqi elite had realized before the 1991 Gulf War. Everyone involved was under enormous psychological pressure not to be duped again, and it was for that reason that everyone, from UN weapons inspectors to the U.S. intelligence community to their French and Russian counterparts, assumed that Saddam Hussein had more capabilities than the inspections were able to uncover. After the 2003 invasion the world learned that the regime was incompetent, corrupt, and compartmentalized to the point where many senior Iraqi officials (including, at times, Saddam himself) believed their country possessed WMD capabilities that did not in fact exist. Before the invasion, though, it would have taken a brave (or foolhardy) intelligence analyst to aggressively downplay the danger represented by Iraq's WMD programs. One who did, Scott Ritter, had his motives severely impugned.

It is, of course, not possible to anticipate all the possible low-probability events that may litter world history in coming months and years. And even if one could anticipate many different futures, it would be impossible to hedge against all of them. Hedging is usually an expensive strategy in which high opportunity costs forsaken have to be weighed against other alternatives. So how does one deal practically with the problem of being blindsided?

This volume is organized into five sections. The first, of which this chapter is a part, introduces the book and examines the fact that surprise is, almost by definition, a psychological problem. Richard Posner, author of *Catastrophe*, observes, for example, that even though one can show that it would be cost-effective to hedge against a low-probability event like an asteroid strike, policymakers and the politicians who hire them are unwilling to pay the cost because they simply cannot imagine such a contingency becoming real.[1] It often takes a Hollywood movie or a similar event occurring in a different country to enable people to visualize a contingency and thus to act on it.

Important institutional constraints, moreover, make it difficult to act even when some people can and do accurately anticipate a low-probability, high-impact contingency. One might call this a form of "socio-surprise" characteristic of collective psychologies. Hurricane Katrina, for example, was one of the most fully predictable and scenario-tested natural disasters in American history, but that fact still did not lead to appropriate preparatory actions or adequate crisis responses on the part of responsible officials at the local, state, or federal levels.

The following section, "Cases: Looking Back," looks more closely at some historical examples of surprise—upside as well as downside—and asks why the social and economic impacts of emergent technologies and events like the collapse of the former Soviet Union and the 1997–98 Asian financial crisis were not anticipated. David Landes, Bruce Berkowitz, and David Hale draw on their knowledge of history and policy to pinpoint those institutional, and not just personal, failures that prevented policymakers and others from properly anticipating major events of the time.

The third section discusses potential future cases of surprise. William Bonvillian, director of MIT's Washington office, suggests ways to set up institutions so that they can deliberately create surprises—positive surprises—in this case for dealing with energy technology and policy issues. Based on the connected-science model that led to applied scientific advances during World War II and thereafter to the establishment and flourishing of DARPA (Defense Advanced Research Projects Agency), Dr. Bonvillian teases out the essence of effective innovation systems. He then applies this essence to what a DARPA-like innovation-generating agency would look like if applied to energy technology. The section also includes chapters by Gal Luft and Anne Korin on other aspects of energy policy, and by Scott Barrett on the uncertainties and dangers concerning new, potentially global-scale diseases.

For reasons rehearsed by Richard Posner, it is clear that psychological preparedness for low-probability events—even ones generated on purpose—is both extremely important, and extremely difficult to achieve. The next section, "Forecasting," tackles this problem.

It is not possible to anticipate all possible futures or to hedge against even a small proportion of them. The incentives to do so are not always present either. After all, politicians need to get reelected in the near term and therefore seldom have the incentive to worry about costs that will be incurred after they have departed the stage. Yet there are nonetheless systematic ways of looking at the future. One is through traditional cost-benefit analysis of the sort Posner outlines, but with proper discounting of future costs and opportunities. Another way of approaching the problem is through scenario methodology. This section thus begins with an essay by Peter Schwartz and Doug Randall of Global Business Network.

Peter Schwartz, whose career started in Royal Dutch/Shell's planning division, has built a business model and career around scenario planning. He observed many years ago that if one proceeded on the basis of a straightforward rational choice model in which one thought through different futures and assigned probability weights to them, senior decisionmakers would simply stop thinking about the low-probability ones. The chief problem is to overcome the psychological resistance to thinking about low-probability futures; the company he created, Global Business Network, has engaged in scenario planning that deliberately ignores probabilities to do precisely that. The focus, Schwartz and Randall argue, needs to be on the decisionmakers themselves and on the institutional constraints they face that allow them to avoid thinking creatively about the future. In this volume, they reflect on the experience of scenario planning over the past two decades.

Another way of thinking systematically is to select hedges, as Robert Lempert recommends in his essay, that are robust over the largest number of possible futures. Like Schwartz and Randall, he is interested in how scenario methodologies can help policymakers find the proper balance between boldness and care in their planning functions.

Technological change has driven much economic and political change. No wonder, then, that technological forecasting has become a staple of our world. And yet even with skillful cost-benefit analysis and scenario techniques, technological forecasters continue to get most things wrong, failing to anticipate major trends and overestimating the importance of the "latest great thing." Could this be because political and economic change also drives technological change, that while technologists are reading the tea leaves from left to right, reality is proceeding from right to left? Why technology forecasting is so poor and why it will probably continue to be poor is the subject of the essay by Mitchell Waldrop, who uses innovation in information technology as his base example to explain why forecasting is so difficult to get right.

The Blindside conference took to heart the very nature of the subject, which calls attention to the cognitive challenges of dealing with low-probability events and so put a premium on getting beyond the usual solipsistic habits of academe. As the program itself featured a debate and two discussions-in-the-round, so those events are represented in this book. The final section, "What Could Be," begins with an edited transcript of a debate between James Kurth of Swarthmore College and Gregg Easterbrook of the Brookings Institution on what may fairly be called the philosophy of forecasting. Kurth uses his wide-ranging intellect to creatively join developments in the geopolitical and spiritual realms and spin out a gloomy prognosis for a declining West. Easterbrook, drawing on his book *The Progress Paradox*, points out that those who look to the facts, rather than to their fears and instincts, will find that the world has been getting better by any number of measures and is likely to continue doing so.[2]

The second and third chapters of the section feature discussions by members of *The American Interest*'s editorial board, dealing in turn with international and American scenarios for low-probability, high-impact events to come. Both the debate and the two discussions evoked novel observations that no one participant would likely have hit upon alone.

There is no easy or obvious methodology that will prevent us from being blindsided in the future. It is important, however, to understand the specific obstacles, both psychological and institutional, that prevent us from first seeing the future clearly and then acting on our insights in a responsible way. The essays in this volume lay out the conceptual problem of anticipating unexpected events, provide glimpses of different possible futures across a range of regions and issues, and may even offer up some creatively practical advice about how to plan for those futures. It is to this kind of creative thinking that *The American Interest* is dedicated.

2

Thinking about Catastrophe

Richard A. Posner

A catastrophe, as I use the term, is an unexpected event that causes great harm. The two parts of the definition fit logically because most harmful events that are expected can be mitigated by preventive measures, often or at least sometimes rendering them less than catastrophic. As science advances, enabling greater predictive accuracy at least over the natural world, scientists may be able to predict catastrophes that cannot be prevented (as well as prevent some man-made catastrophes that cannot be predicted). So to be more precise, let me substitute for "unexpected event" the phrase "event of low or unknown probability"—that is, an event that is either low-risk or uncertain, in the statisticians' useful distinction between risk and uncertainty.

Catastrophes have been common enough in human history, and there is no paradox in describing as "common" a series of events of low or unknown probability. That is because the very low probabilities of a very large number of possibilities can aggregate to a probability close to 1. But—and here *is* a paradox—the problem of dealing with catastrophes has gotten bigger simply because the range of catastrophes that cannot be averted or mitigated has gotten smaller. Until recently, for example, there was no reason to worry about an asteroid strike because nothing could be done to prevent it and little if anything could be done to mitigate its effects. Now, by careful mapping of the orbits of asteroids whose orbits intercept Earth's orbit, and by skillful deployment of rockets to nudge dangerous asteroids out of their current orbits, catastrophic asteroid strikes can be prevented.[1] Early-warning systems for tsunamis are now available, as well. So now the question is whether to take these defensive measures, given that the required investment of human and technical resources could also be used elsewhere. The larger the number of preventable catastrophes that are identified, the more difficult the issue of resource allocation becomes.

The march of science is doing something else: It is creating *more* catastrophic risks. This is obvious in the case of modern weapons of mass destruction, but it is also happening in more esoteric areas of scientific advance such as genetically modified crops, nanotechnology, and robotics. Sheer economic and population growth is doing its share, too, by contributing to global warming but also by making certain places more vulnerable to catastrophe and by making weapons of mass destruction more affordable. As to vulnerability, the August-September 2005 flooding of New Orleans was a consequence in part of economic development that had eliminated natural barriers to flooding. As to affordability, there is a particularly sinister conjunction with respect to biological weapons, because they are becoming cheaper at the same time that they are becoming more lethal and that people and nations are becoming wealthier. The Unabomber attacked with letter bombs; a biological Unabomber with bioengineering skills may soon be able to attack with aerosols of synthesized smallpox virus.

On top of all this, geopolitical changes, in conjunction with the increased availability of such weapons, are increasing the likelihood of catastrophic attacks. Here I refer specifically to the rise of global terrorism with apocalyptic aims and suicidal means that preclude effective deterrence, the growing instability and hostility (to the West and its allies) of the vast Muslim world, and the emergence of heavily armed "rogue states," notably (at the moment) Iran and North Korea.

In sum, there are many more catastrophic risks that we can productively worry about than ever before: more risks, and a greater proportion of preventable risks. This is an uncomfortable situation for three fundamental reasons, one psychological, a second political, and a third analytical.

Psychological Discomforts

The psychological problem is the difficulty of getting people, even most officials and many intellectually gifted people, to think seriously about catastrophes that have not yet happened. It takes no imagination to think seriously and productively about airplane crashes, forest fires, cardiac arrest, and other common catastrophes (large or small), because these things happen frequently enough to make them part of ordinary experience. In other words, these events do not need to be *imagined*. But thinking that absolutely requires imagination is another matter altogether.

This observation has implications that are often underestimated. Imagination is a very scarce resource, and also a highly imperfect one, because thinking about things that have not happened is inherently more difficult than thinking about things that have. For one thing, probabilities—things that may or may not happen—are far more difficult to estimate than frequencies—things that will happen sooner or later. With probabilities, too, the human imagination is quickly overwhelmed because, while only a finite number of things *has* happened, the range of things that *may* happen is literally infinite. It is impossible for an individual, a government, or even a supercomputer to think about an infinite number of things. So the larger the array of possible preventable catastrophes, the more there is to think about, implying heavy demand and potential exhaustion of the imagination capacity of the society.

This problem of cognitive overload is exacerbated—and here I verge into the political impediments to responding to catastrophic risks—by the fact that the human mind has great difficulty thinking in probabilistic terms, especially when the probabilities are low. This is a problem not of having to think about too many things at once, but of having to think about one thing that is of low or unknown probability. Human brains did not evolve to deal easily with such events because in the ancestral environment, as evolutionary biologists call it, when human brains assumed their approximate current structure, there was no payoff to being quick-witted about probabilistic events about which one could do very little or nothing. A large and convincing literature in cognitive psychology shows that nonexperts handle probabilistic dangers very badly, sometimes exaggerating them unreasonably but more often writing them down to zero, that is, ignoring them.[2]

In a democratic society, the reactions of nonexperts, that is, of ordinary people, have a significant impact on public policy. President George W. Bush's science adviser once told me that while he appreciated that asteroid strikes were a menace that might justify a greater investment of national resources in detection and prevention, the investment would not be made because the American people simply do not worry about asteroid strikes, even though such a strike could, depending on the size of the asteroid, do incalculable damage up to and including the extinction of the human race.

Political Obstacles

The political obstacles to responding intelligently to catastrophic risks are magnified by the short horizons of politicians and many of their constituents. The probability of an event is a function of the time interval under consideration. A biological attack on the United States is much more likely within the next ten years than within the next week, and is less likely (though this is little more than a guess) within the next six months than an unfavorable outcome of the war in Iraq. So the natural tendency is to focus more on the war than on the threat of a biological attack. Likewise, if global warming is not likely to cause serious harm for another century or so, as many scientists believe (though there is some unknown danger of earlier, abrupt climate change), politicians are unlikely to take costly measures to combat it even if deferring the measures would greatly increase the harm. Civil servants often have longer horizons than politicians, but not much longer.

Politicians and civil servants are not the only ones with truncated horizons; ordinary individuals have them, as well. Their horizons are longer (as politicians' horizons would be if political office were hereditary) because of altruism toward one's children and grandchildren and perhaps even remoter descendants. But they are not infinite, which means that neither the current generation nor its political representatives internalize the welfare of remote unborn generations.

Some of the political obstacles to responding effectively to catastrophe can be more fully appreciated by examining the tsunami that ravaged the coastline of the Indian Ocean in December 2004. Suppose that a tsunami of that destructiveness occurs on average once a century and kills 250,000 people. That is an average of 2,500 deaths a year. Even without attempting a sophisticated estimate of the value of life to the people exposed to the risk, one can say with some confidence that if an annual death toll of 2,500 could be substantially reduced at a moderate annual cost, the investment would be worthwhile. A combination of educating the residents of low-lying coastal areas about the warning signs of a tsunami (tremors and a sudden recession in the ocean); establishing a warning system involving emergency broadcasts, telephoned warnings, and air-raid-type sirens; and improving emergency response systems would have saved many of the people killed by the Indian Ocean tsunami, probably at a total cost below any reasonable estimate of the average losses that can be expected from tsunamis. Relocating people away from coasts would be even more efficacious, but except in the most vulnerable areas or in areas in which residential or commercial uses have only marginal value, the costs would probably exceed the benefits because annual costs of protection must be matched with annual, not total, expected costs of tsunamis.

So why were such systems not in place when the 2004 tsunami struck? First, although a once-in-a-century event is *as* likely to occur at the beginning of the century as at any other time, it is much *less* likely to occur during the first decade of the century than at some time in the last nine. Politicians with limited terms of office and thus foreshortened political horizons tend to discount low-risk disaster possibilities steeply because the risk of damage to their careers from failing to take precautionary measures is truncated.

Second, to the extent that effective precautions require governmental action, the fact that government is a centralized system of control makes it difficult for officials to respond to the full spectrum of possible risks against which cost-justified measures might be taken. Given the variety of matters to which they must attend, senior officials are likely to have a high threshold of attention below which risks are simply ignored (and the more senior they are, the higher the threshold). The upper levels of the U.S. government, preoccupied with terrorist threats, paid insufficient attention to the risk of a disastrous flood in New Orleans, even though the risk was understood to be significant.

Third, where risks are regional or global rather than local, many national governments, especially in poorer and smaller countries, may drag their heels in the hope of taking a free ride on larger and richer countries. Knowing this, and not wishing to reward and thus encourage free riding, the richer countries may be reluctant to take precautionary measures. Again, there is a U.S. parallel: State and local governments may stint on devoting resources to emergency response, expecting aid from other state and local governments and the federal government.

Fourth, countries are poor often because of weak, inefficient, or corrupt government, characteristics that may disable poor nations from taking cost-justified precautions. Again there is a U.S. parallel: Louisiana is a poor state and New Orleans, which has a large poor population, has a reputation for having an inefficient and corrupt government.

And fifth, the positive correlation of per capita income with value of life (see below) suggests that it is rational (though not always easy to explain as such) for even a well-governed poor country to devote proportionately fewer resources to averting calamities than rich countries do. This would also be true of a poor state or city in the United States.

Unfortunately, some of these political problems afflict not only poor countries, states, and cities; they afflict the mighty U. S. federal government as well, as the Hurricane Katrina debacle illustrates.[3] Set aside for a moment (I return to the point later) the question whether the levees should have been strengthened or other measures taken to reduce the risk of a major flood; that is the analytical question. For current purposes the important point is that such measures were not taken. Hence the risk of such a flood was not eliminated; this was known (a 2002 series in the New Orleans *Times-Picayune* had explained the risk of a disastrous flood in the city in great detail[4]); and it followed that it might be necessary to respond to such a flood. Yet four years after 9/11, and two and a half years after the creation of the Department of Homeland Security, the federal government had yet to devise an executable plan for responding to a catastrophic event in New Orleans, or, I imagine, in any other threatened city in the United States. (I had thought Washington, D.C., was an exception, but it turns out it was not and is not.)[5]

Now, this failure *seems* incomprehensible. Planning an evacuation would not have been costly. It would not even have stepped on any big political toes. The need for emergency planning was not only apparent; it was explicitly acknowledged at every level of officialdom. So why did nothing happen? One reason I have already discussed is that a democratic (perhaps any) government is incapable of taking effective measures against novel threats. They do not have to be *really* novel; it is enough that no major American city had recently been inundated. The human mind, as already noted, has trouble thinking in terms of probabilities as distinct from frequencies, and politicians have foreshortened horizons (the probability of a disastrous flood in New Orleans was less than 10 percent over a period of thirty years, far longer than a politician's horizon). Policy myopia is thus built into democratic politics and is aggravated by the rapid turnover of appointed officials as they cycle between public sector and private sector jobs. An official who spends only two years in a job is unlikely to worry about what may happen decades hence. He will receive no current benefit from planning to deal with contingencies, however ominous, that seem to lie in the remote future.

Another obstacle to responding effectively to catastrophic risk is the pressure of the immediate. Officials are continuously harassed by members of Congress, the media, and White House staff to deal with the crisis du jour. They are not given leisure to address future contingencies, even to the extent of planning for them. Most of the offices in the federal government that are formally charged with conducting long-range planning do very little of it, in part because senior policymakers, with their truncated horizons and urgent distractions, do not pay serious attention to such planning efforts. The problem is aggravated by the sheer number of possible catastrophes, which makes it difficult to think systematically about responding.

Another obstacle, though this one is limited to after-the-fact as distinct from preventive responses, is cultural. Americans are not fatalists. They accept, for example, that national defense requires reserve forces and standby resources such as manned missile silos. But they would find it difficult to understand the use of government funds to establish a standby disaster command whose members sit around waiting for Seattle to be engulfed in a volcanic eruption by Mount Rainier or New Orleans to be inundated by a storm surge. Americans accept the inevitability of evil, but not of disaster.

And then there is the deficient *political* culture (in part a consequence of the social culture) that has produced the Department of Homeland Security in its current form. The creation of the department in 2003 was among a number of responses to the need to "do something" in the wake of the September 11, 2001, terrorist attacks. The need for better coordination of the numerous agencies responsible for protecting the nation's borders, and of the agencies that have responsibilities for responding to catastrophes, whether natural or man-made, was real enough. After all, America's three main border agencies—the Border Patrol, the Customs Service, and the Coast Guard—were located in three different executive departments (Justice, Treasury, and Transportation, respectively) and were incapable of effective coordination on any level. But that did not justify placing twenty-two agencies, including the Federal Emergency Management Agency (FEMA), a heretofore independent agency reporting directly to the president, in a gigantic new department. The department is centrally managed, hierarchical, with information flowing upward from the brontosaurus's tail to its tiny head (a handful of people, albeit some very able, trying to control more than 180,000 civil servants), and a response groping its way back down.

With the department's formation, FEMA was effectively demoted in the governmental hierarchy, losing much of its perceived importance in the process. Appointments to its senior managerial jobs could now be used to pay small political debts—and for the further reason that emergency response, though a challenging specialty, is not yet a formal profession like medicine or law, so there is a less definite sense of the proper credentials for the officials.[6] And now FEMA had to stand in line, waiting its turn for the attention of the beleaguered secretary of Homeland Security, who was struggling to assert control over his new far-flung domain. A plan formulated by FEMA for responding to large-scale catastrophe would have to be approved not only by the White House (which has its own Homeland Security Council, whose role in the response to Hurricane Katrina remains obscure), but also by the Secretary of Homeland Security. And the secretary was unlikely to be an expert in emergency response, given the breadth of his responsibilities. But this meant that when disaster struck, the head of FEMA, an amateur in emergency response because the job was no longer considered very important, the agency having dropped a rung in the hierarchy of government agencies, had to consult a higher official, also an amateur in emergency response.

There was another problem with sticking FEMA in an immense new department. The department's emphasis was on fighting terrorism, and so preparing to deal with natural disasters got sidetracked, even though both natural and terrorist disasters can require similar responses.[7] This illustrates how placing a bureaucratic layer over heretofore independent agencies can undermine efforts to prevent catastrophes. The people at the top have a limited span of attention and control and so may be inclined to focus on a single mission, thereby curtailing the spectrum of risks that are dealt with.

What I am calling a deficient political culture is in part a result of the "do something" attitude of a nation of nonfatalists but probably in greater part a result of the interaction between a decentralized government structure designed in the eighteenth century and the enormous challenges to government thrust upon it by the complexity and diversity of modern America and its position in the world. The separation of the legislative and executive branches (which are effectively fused in a parliamentary system, such as that of the United Kingdom), aggressive judiciaries, and the distribution of government power among federal agencies, the states, and local governments make timely and coherent government action difficult at best, and perhaps impossible in dealing with subtle novel challenges.

Analytical Problems

The analytical problem of dealing effectively with catastrophic risks lies in the limitations of cost-benefit analysis. A cost-benefit analysis is the rational way to determine what if anything to do about the risk of something bad happening. In a simple analysis, first multiply the cost of the event if it materializes (say, a flood) by the probability that it will materialize if no (or no additional) preventive measures are taken. That will give the expected cost of the bad event. Next, calculate the cost of the measures necessary to prevent the event from occurring (that is, to eliminate the risk) and compare the two figures. If the expected cost of the event exceeds the cost of prevention (a cost measured by the value that the resources used for prevention would earn in their best alternative employment), adopt the measures. So, for example, say there is a 1 percent chance of a flood that would cause $1 billion in damages, making the expected cost of the flood $10 million, and also assume the cost of averting the flood would be $9 million. As a first approximation, the preventive measure should be adopted. (It is only a first approximation because one must consider whether that $9 million might be invested even more productively elsewhere, of which more below.) A slight complication is that the measure may reduce rather than eliminate the risk; in that case, the reduction in expected cost is what is to be compared with the cost of (partial) prevention, that is, risk reduction.

Cost-benefit analysis of responding to catastrophic risk is often feasible. The flood caused by Hurricane Katrina is an example. In 1998 it was estimated that preventing such a flood would cost $14 billion; the estimated "economic" cost (that is, ignoring loss of life and physical and emotional suffering) of the flood was estimated at $100 billion–$200 billion;[8] and the Army Corps of Engineers estimated the annual probability of such a flood at 1 in 300.[9] Taking the lower cost and assuming that the $14 billion investment would eliminate the probability of a flood within thirty years—a period in which the probability of a flood (if the measures were not taken) would be a shade under 10 percent—yields an expected benefit from the flood-control measures of $10 billion. The proposed measures therefore flunked a cost-benefit test, since $10 billion is less than $14 billion.

They should not have flunked. The calculation of future benefits ignored the fact that the benefits are likely to grow—a flood that occurred thirty years hence would be likely to do more damage because property values would have increased—although these enhanced future benefits would have to be discounted to present value. Worse, the analysis ignored the expected loss of life, and other human suffering, that a massive flood would cause. There is a substantial economic literature inferring the value of life from the costs people are willing to incur to avoid small risks of death; if from behavior toward risk one infers that a person would pay $70 to avoid a 1-in-100,000 risk of death, his value of life would be estimated at $7 million ($70/.00001), which is in fact the median estimate of the value of life of an American. (These estimates are sensitive to incomes, as I noted earlier; the less money people have, the less they will allocate toward minimizing risks of death, which will automatically depress the measured value of life.)

The utility of this transformation is simply that, once a risk is calculated, its expected cost is instantly derived simply by multiplying the risk by the value of life. But a more intuitive way to understand the "value of life" estimates is as a summation of the value that people place on avoiding slight risks. A 1-in-100,000 risk of death implies that if 100,000 people are exposed to the risk, 1 will die. If each of the 100,000 would demand $70 to bear the 1-in-100,000 risk of death, then the total demanded would be $7 million, and we can simply call this, for simplicity's sake, the value of the life of the 1 person who did die.

Now, the method just outlined—call it classic cost-benefit analysis—for dealing rationally with potential adversity unfortunately tends to break down in catastrophic situations. The stumbling blocks include difficulties in estimating probabilities (less commonly in estimating costs and benefits), in prioritizing risks, and in discounting for futurity; these are apart from the cognitive (and other psychological) and political factors discussed above.

Two common confusions need first to be dispelled. The first is that all catastrophic risks are low-probability events; the second is that public policy should focus on high-probability events, such as heart attacks.

Statisticians distinguish between risk and uncertainty. A risk is a contingent event to which a numerical probability can be assigned; a contingent event is uncertain if no probability can be assigned. When someone says that he is much more likely to die of a heart attack than be killed by a terrorist, he is implicitly assigning a low probability to a terrorist attack. That is a mistake; the probability of such an attack cannot be determined. Terrorist attacks have been infrequent causes of death, relative to heart attacks, in the past, but there is no basis for thinking that the future of terrorism will be similar to its past.

Even if it were known that terrorist attacks would continue to be infrequent and to inflict relatively limited damage (relative to the damage that would be inflicted, say, by a terrorist attack with weapons of mass destruction), it would not follow that resources should be reallocated from the struggle against terrorism to the struggle against heart disease. Probability is not the only factor in cost-benefit analysis. Considering the average age of heart-attack victims and the ability to reduce the likelihood of such an attack by modifying one's behavior, society may well already be spending the cost-justified amount of money (or more) on the prevention of heart attacks.

Some catastrophic risks can be quantified: the flooding of New Orleans is one example, and another is the range of possible asteroid collisions, about which a fair amount is known because of the long geological history of the earth and the moon. But for most catastrophes, risks cannot be estimated; some cannot even be bounded (except between 0 and 1!). Those are the cases of genuine uncertainty in the statistician's sense.

If one cannot estimate risk, one cannot do cost-benefit analysis. But that does not leave us completely stymied. Two remedial techniques merit more widespread use. One I call "inverse cost-benefit analysis." It involves calculating the *implied* risk from data on the cost of the catastrophe if it occurs and on the amount of money currently being spent to avert the risk of its occurring.

Catastrophe (deaths)	*Costs being spent to reduce risk*	*Loss if risk materalizes*	*Probability that it will materialize (implied)*
Bioterrorist attack (100 million)	$2 billion	$1 quadrillion (U.S. loss only)	.000002 (1 in 500,000)
Asteroid collision (1.5 billion)	$3.9 million	$3 quadrillion	.0000000013 (1 in 769 million)
Strangelet disaster in particle accelerator	$0	$600 trillion	0
Catastrophic global warming	$1.7 billion	$66.6 trillion (U.S. loss only)	.00000255 (1 in 388,000)

That is, if the government is spending $1 million on trying to prevent a catastrophe that, if it occurs, will cause damage of $100 million, the implication is that the government reckons the risk of the catastrophe as 1 percent or less, since the expected cost of a 1 percent risk of a $100 million loss is $1 million. If the real risk is higher and could be averted by an additional expenditure less than that added risk, the government is underspending. This explanation is a little oversimplified, but it will do to illustrate the potential utility of the technique. The table, taken from my book *Catastrophe*, shows how application of the technique strongly suggests government underspending.

Another technique for approximating cost-benefit analysis under conditions of uncertainty goes by the name "tolerable windows" and is illustrated in the figure. The marginal benefits (*mb*) and marginal costs (*mc*) of measures to reduce or eliminate some catastrophic risk are shown as functions of the quantity of precautions taken, with the optimal level of precautions (q^*) given by the intersection of the two functions. Suppose the optimum cannot be determined because of uncertainty about costs, benefits, the discount rate, or probabilities. Nevertheless enough may be known about the benefits and costs to be able to create the "window" formed by the two vertical lines.[10] Notice that

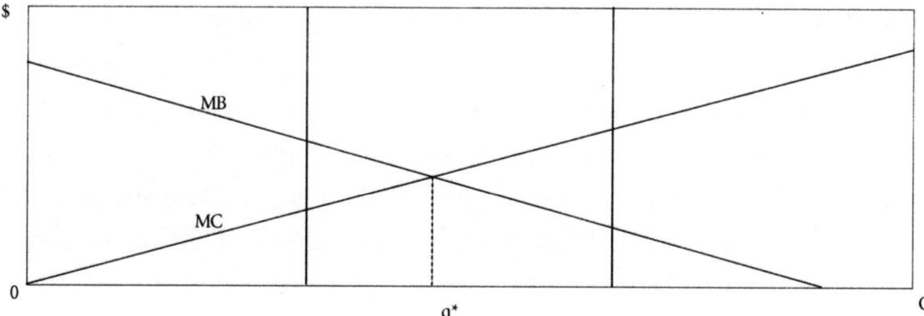

at the left side of the window frame, the benefits of a further effort to eliminate or prevent the catastrophe in question comfortably exceed the costs, while at the right side costs exceed benefits. Staying within the window gives some basis for confidence that the measures, while they may not be optimal, are neither grossly inadequate nor grossly excessive. This technique might be plausibly applied to the current funding of asteroid defense—which is probably well to the left of the left side of the window.

Using cost-benefit analysis to design optimal responses to catastrophic risks presents a priorities problem that arises from the infinite number of such risks. By discussing just a few, I have made the analytical task seem simpler than it is. Suppose the number of catastrophic risks worth worrying about, considering their magnitude and the feasibility of reducing them, is set at 100; even if preventive measures for each of them pass a cost-benefit test, it will be unclear how many of those measures should actually be adopted, since their benefits have to be compared with the benefits of alternative use of resources, uses that may have nothing to do with catastrophes. Policymakers could impoverish the country and the world by focusing excessively on eliminating catastrophic risks.

A partial answer is that the catastrophic risks tend to come in clusters from a prevention or response standpoint. Many of the measures for preventing or mitigating a bioterror attack will also prevent or mitigate a natural epidemic. An evacuation plan for a city such as Seattle, San Francisco, or New Orleans that is vulnerable to a natural disaster will also serve if the city is the victim of a WMD attack. Measures to reduce demand for oil will both alleviate (though I fear only slightly) global warming and reduce the likelihood of a catastrophic energy shortage resulting from our dependence on unstable and potentially hostile oil-exporting nations.

Finally as to the problem of discounting: If there is a temporal mismatch between costs and benefits, discounting will be required to enable a cost-benefit analysis to be conducted. The benefits of eliminating a catastrophic risk consist of the benefits of eliminating, say, a 1 percent chance of a flood this year, a 1 percent chance of a flood next year, and so on indefinitely. The probability of an event tends to rise with the interval over which the probability is assessed. The probability that an event with a 1 percent annual probability of occurring will in fact occur over the next century is not 100 percent but is close to it. This means that most of the expected cost of the event will lie in the future, perhaps the very distant future, even if the *annual* probability stays the same. If society values the future less than the present, the sum of the benefits of eliminating the risk will thus be smaller than simply the multiple of the first-year benefits and the number of years the risk is expected to persist if nothing is done about it.

So the question becomes how heavily to weight expected costs that will be borne in the distant future. In noncommercial settings, as where one is trying to decide what weight to give to the expected cost of a tsunami in the third millennium, there is no intellectually satisfying answer. The only remotely satisfactory approach goes by the name "limited horizons."

To understand what is meant by "limited horizons," consider that the present value of an infinite stream of costs discounted at 4 percent is equal to the undiscounted sum of those costs for twenty-five years, while the present value of an infinite stream of costs discounted at 1 percent is equal to the undiscounted sum of those costs for one hundred years. So one might argue for the 4 percent rate (that is, for truncating concern for future welfare at twenty-five years) by saying that the current generation is willing to weight the welfare of the next generation as heavily as its own welfare, but that is the extent of its regard for the future. Or one might argue for the 1 percent rate by saying that the current generation is willing to give equal weight to the welfare of everyone living in this century—including themselves, their children, and their grandchildren—but beyond that they don't care. Looking at future welfare in this way, one may incline toward the lower rate—which would have dramatic implications for the willingness to invest today in limiting global warming. The lower rate could even be regarded as a ceiling.

After all, most people have some regard for human welfare, or at least the survival of some human civilization, in future centuries. We ought to be grateful that the Romans did not try to exterminate the human race in chagrin at the impending collapse of their empire. Since we owe future generations something like that consideration, we simply cannot afford in this day and age not to think about catastrophic risks. But thinking about them is very difficult, doing something practical about them even more so. Society therefore faces a great challenge, to which it had better rise. There cannot be any assurance that policymakers will heed cost-benefit analyses that reveal clear and substantial benefits from measures of prevention or mitigation of catastrophic risks. Such analyses are not a sufficient condition of wise policy, but they are probably a necessary condition.

Part I

Cases: Looking Back

3 Slow Surprise: The Dynamics of Technology Synergy

David Landes

Surprise in human life comes in many forms and time frames. When the first mosquito of the season in the back yard surprises a person, who slaps at his ankle in reaction, the entire episode can be measured in just a second. Military surprises affecting entire societies, like the Japanese assault on Pearl Harbor and the September 11 attacks, are events that typically unfold within a day or days, even though weeks or months may have gone into secret preparations. Surprises in the economic domain, such as a major recession or a deep regional financial crisis, emerge over a still longer period—weeks and months, with traceable repercussions that may last for years.

The psychological meaning of surprise, therefore, is very much dependent on its context. If one were still surprised by that mosquito a half hour after the event, that would be odd. If a person stopped being surprised, on reflection, about the way the cold war ended, so quickly in relative terms and without a shot being fired, that would also be odd, but for entirely different reasons—for that surprise is based not on a simple and immediate sensory reaction but on an array of expectations of a far more abstract kind.

Beyond military, geopolitical, and economic surprises are surprises that emerge even more slowly—those that seem surprises only in what might be called deep retrospect. To understand what "slow surprise" comes to when one contemplates phenomena that unfurl not over seconds or weeks or months or even years, but over a decade or more, one has to step back farther than usual to acquire the right perspective. That is what has to be done in discussing the history and sociology of science and technology. For that purpose, in staking out the farther reaches of the "blindside" concept, technological surprises must be considered not by looking at what seems most novel in the last few issues of *Nature*, for example; it would be impossible properly to understand their impact, for the simple reason that there has not yet been an impact. One can look back to some major advance that shaped the world of the twentieth century and that, by the way (but not entirely incidentally), produced the essential backdrop against which pivotal surprises of shorter gestation periods occurred. This big and slow surprise arose from an unexpected (from the vantage point of one century ago) combination of scientific and technological change: the automobile, oil, and electricity—the interrelated triple surprise of the early twentieth century.

Lord, Mr. Ford, What Have You Done?

Some several years ago the editors of the *New York Times* invited some people to write essays on major innovators, the people who, in the estimation of those invited to write, did most to change the world we live in. I was invited and chose to write about Henry Ford. The editors rejected the essay because, they said, they did not like my choice of subject. They did not like Henry Ford. I do not blame them for that; I did not—and still do not—like Henry Ford either. He was, among other things, an obnoxious and active anti-Semite, vicious and irrational even in his own generation. Still, I was right and the *New York Times* was wrong on the merits, for the same reason that *Time* magazine has over the years rightly selected quite odious candidates for their "person of the year." The criterion set forth is not general popularity but impact. Henry Ford did more to change the material world than any person of his era: He made the automobile an available necessity. And that was a surprise that virtually no one who was present at the invention of the automobile expected.

In the early days the automobile was the story of an expensive toy, something to play with, perhaps in competition. Ford himself was a racing car driver. The automobile then developed into a luxury substitute for horses or for horses and carriages. There was a multitude of automakers: hundreds of them, each making an individualistic product to suit the desires and tastes of its customers. To be sure, the constraints of technology, plus visual and performance characteristics, led irresistibly to standardization. But the auto was complicated enough to provide plenty of opportunity for variation, especially for what was overwhelmingly at first a well-to-do clientele.

Such was the social and economic location and role of the automobile in its early years, but Henry Ford changed all that. His contribution lay in his sense of superior technical judgment, which freed him of the need to cater to customers' tastes. "They can have any color they want," Ford famously said, "so long as it's black." The result was the cheapest of standardized cars, made of standardized parts fabricated through techniques of mass production. Some of this mass production entailed a sacrifice of quality at customer cost in both money and safety.

This was a basic manufacturing choice whose implications endured for many years. Remember the Ford Pinto of the 1970s and 1980s? This was one downstream consequence of Ford's efforts to economize by making body parts serve more than one purpose. Thus, the top of the Pinto's gas tank was also used as the bottom of the rear seat, and this, I don't have to tell you, gave rise to an unusually high frequency of fiery fatal accidents. The Ford Motor Company ended up paying lots of money to victims who had the good sense and the awareness—and were lucky enough still to be alive—to go to a lawyer and sue the Ford Company. As it happened, the company had already calculated what it might cost to pay the victims of the Pinto technique, and this showed that the Ford Motor Company saved more thereby than it paid out. The company did not begin to behave differently until new federal rules forbade auto manufacturers to do that kind of thing.

Ford, of course, was not alone in moving toward standardization and cheaper—meaning of lesser quality and greater affordability—automobiles. Its greatest competition came from companies like General Motors, which made a range of vehicles aiming at a range of incomes and uses. For several years in the 1920s and 1930s, Ford was making more or less one kind of car. General Motors put itself forward as the manufacturer of a variety of cars that would appeal to a broad range of American buyers. William Durant, the visionary who dreamed of an auto company selling to a stratified market, once tried to sell a banker (J. P. Morgan himself) on his dream of auto success. Durant predicted hundreds of thousands of cars on the road in a matter of a few years. Morgan threw him out of his office.

Well, Durant was right and Morgan was wrong. But Morgan kept his money and Durant lost a fortune. It was his successor, Alfred P. Sloan, and the DuPont representatives, who made General Motors the biggest car company in the world. Ford remained second.

Now the success of the auto rested on more than simple carriage building and marketing insights. Most people could still do better relying on trains, subways, and trolleys to get around. Even if they could afford an automobile in some absolute sense, that did not make it the wisest transportation choice for most people, especially in cities. The auto won its buyers by improvements in engines, starters, steering systems, tires, bodies, and fuel. These improvements made the difference between self-reliance and dependence on chauffeurs. This does not occur to most of us today; it is a surprise to grasp the fact that the kind of people who could afford an auto early in the twentieth century could afford a chauffeur, too. A manufacturer who wanted to sell lots of autos to ordinary middle-class American drivers had to devise improvements that made it easy to start a car, easy to steer it, easy to stop it, and easy to fix it.

Now to do this, it was necessary to have widely available a variety of components and materials: petroleum, electrical batteries, rubber, and steel. And the auto was both the beneficiary of these components in its rise to becoming a necessity, and a generator of them, as well. This brings us to the second of our three connected surprises: petroleum.

Black Gold

Petroleum went way back, of course. The pillar of fire the Israelites followed upon their exodus from Egypt was probably petroleum's first introduction into literature, and that was a very long time ago. At first petroleum's value was for illumination and lubrication, including its form as paraffin wax. That is how things remained through the third quarter of the nineteenth century. Fuel uses followed, however, and that changed everything.

The use of petroleum for fuel did not start with automobiles. It started as a fuel for ships at sea, replacing or supplementing coal-fired ships. With the automobile coming along, however, there was now a vehicle ready to use petroleum to drive it. That led to a greater than anticipated demand.

People first found petroleum where they knew it was, for they could see it coming up from the ground. But with the demand furnished by the automobile, people began exploring for petroleum, and they also turned their attention to better ways of extracting, refining, and transporting the product. Indeed, the key technical consideration was the need for refining and transporting, and these, far more than finding supplies, were the basis for great fortunes in this field—including that of the Rockefellers and other petroleum entrepreneurs.

Refining turned out to be the easier of the tasks; the special problem was transport. John D. Rockefeller built his fortune through his control of rail transport. Believe it or not, he missed out at first on pipelines, but he had so much money and economic clout that when he eventually realized his mistake, he could still take over the pipeline oil industry. Meanwhile, the invention of the auto changed completely the significance and value of the petroleum industry. And in time, of course, motor vehicles as much and then more than rail transport ended up taking care of the petroleum transport problem—a perfect example of industrial-age symbiosis.

A Family Romance

The third great technological surprise of the early twentieth century was electricity. Electricity was a form of energy that lent itself to the newest and most ingenious devices, as anyone who has ever heard of Thomas Alva Edison is aware. One needs energy to generate electricity, and everyone knows that petroleum can be used to do that. So petroleum became key to both power generation and transportation.

What will come as a surprise to many, however, concerns how people figured out ways to find all the petroleum needed for transportation and power generation, and this is a story that emphasizes the role of luck and brains: what may be called the "Schlumberger Romance."

The Schlumberger Romance starts with a family from Alsace, an early center of European industry. They were a family with carefully considered alliances, of cultivated education and cultivated Calvinist diligence. The Schlumberger family was one of the most successful of a group of such industrial families, and it cultivated ties to the other industrial dynasties of the region: the Japie, the Kirclan, and the Dulfuse. The Schlumbergers built their initial fortune on textiles and then on textile machinery. They were successful builders of the French catch-up to the British Industrial Revolution in the nineteenth century, but politics and war interfered. One branch of the family left Alsace in the 1870s and moved to Paris, the center of French higher education and of the competitive *Grandes Ecoles*. The father had very bright children and high hopes. He sent them to these selective schools, and he offered to finance their careers if they devoted themselves to science and engineering. The subject of his choice: electricity.

The Schlumberger line of experiment and inquiry involved using electrical current to read and predict the content of unseen surfaces, including unseen spaces beneath the earth's surface. The first of these were subsurface areas that could then be checked and verified, for one could not proceed unless one knew if the machines worked. And where better to find out than in the tunnels of the early Paris Metro? So this is what the scions of the Schlumberger family did, and this in time made possible the development of a language of electrical reading, minerals, empty space, geological structures and so forth. This technology turned out to be useful for a variety of purposes. Finding petroleum deposits was not what the Schlumbergers had originally in mind. Nonetheless, that turned out, in distant places, to be the most valuable use of all.

So here are the ingredients of the triple surprise: the vehicle, which needs petroleum; and the way to find and move and refine that petroleum; and electric energy as needed. But then World War II came, Paris again fell to the German invader, and the Schlumbergers fled France to Texas, where they already had oil interests. There they put a son-in-law in charge of the business, most unusual from the French point of view. The son-in-law changed his name from "Jean" to "John," so he could look and sound American; but when he went back to France, he called himself "Jean" again. And he called himself "de Menil," and the "de" told all the French that he was a person of noble extraction—DNA extraction, not oil.

No one could possibly have anticipated the triple surprise a hundred years ago. Sometimes, oftentimes really, surprise is a result not of one line of development taking off in rapid or unexpected directions, but rather the result of a confluence of independent developments that somehow link up. Technological surprise, seen in retrospect, is often a compound as well as a "slow" surprise. It all makes sense when it is seen from today's perspective, but no one could see it looking forward.

This triple surprise has seemed to most people to be a very happy story (except, perhaps, for those people who bought a Pinto). It was a story of progress, affluence, fortunes made, and freedoms won. Alas, despite the successful prospecting pioneered by Schlumberger and others, the number of autos and their energy appetites may now be surpassing the supply of fossil fuel. The twentieth century was the century of the automobile and of Henry Ford, but now the big question is what will be the next surprise, and where will it take us from here? Of course, we cannot possibly know the answer. That is a "slow surprise" in the making for our successors, after all. We wouldn't want to spoil their fun.

4 U.S. Intelligence Estimates of Soviet Collapse: Reality and Perception

Bruce Berkowitz

It is commonly believed that the U.S. intelligence community failed to anticipate the collapse of the Soviet Union. Indeed, many of the U.S. officials who received intelligence about the Soviet Union, its decline in the late 1970s and 1980s, and its final crises in the 1989–91 period, believe to this day that they were not warned—that they were, in effect, "blindsided."

This is odd, because the documented record shows that the intelligence community performed much better than most people seem to think. Indeed, this record suggests that U.S. intelligence provided about as good a product as one could reasonably expect. It detected the slowdown in the Soviet economy; it noted that the Soviet leadership was running out of options to save the country; it stipulated a set of conditions that might signal the crisis had reached a tipping point; and it notified top U.S. leaders when these conditions were met.

So these facts raise two questions: Why do so many people think the intelligence community failed? And why do many of the U.S. officials who were professional consumers of this intelligence still feel that they were not adequately warned? First, however, the nature of these questions should be noted.

In part, the questions are not about empirical realities but about perceptions of those realities. To use a photography metaphor, the questions are asking not about the "picture" out there, but about the "camera" in human heads. As such, the questions are not asking about the external conditions that produce surprise, but rather, the *collective cognitive architecture* of surprise. Put another way, leaders usually do not "get" blindsided; they blindside themselves by how they perceive intelligence, by the mental hurdles intelligence must surmount before it can change their perceptions, and in the constraints that limit their ability to act on information.

The questions are also about wishful thinking. As will be seen, deep down, officials seem to want intelligence to make decisions for them, when, in reality, it rarely can.

The Record, on Background

In 1995 Jeffrey Richelson brought to my attention several intelligence assessments and National Intelligence Estimates (NIEs) that had been declassified and cited in a study that Kirsten Lundberg carried out for the Kennedy School at Harvard.[1] Richelson, a scholar at the National Security Archive, is one of the most frequent users of the Freedom of Information Act (FOIA) and has over the years assembled an extensive database of declassified, leaked, and officially released intelligence products. When Richelson saw the citations in the Kennedy School study, he requested the documents under FOIA.

Richelson realized that these assessments were at odds with the popular conception that the intelligence community had failed to anticipate the collapse of the Soviet Union. The documents, since supplemented by others published by the CIA's Center for the Study of Intelligence, provide a factual basis for evaluating the intelligence community's record. Richelson and I agreed to develop our own assessment of the U.S. intelligence community's performance and to consider how the distorted views of its Soviet analyses had developed. We interviewed most of the officials who participated in developing the analysis and several of the key consumers who served in the White House under George H. W. Bush.[2]

We concluded that the performance of the U.S. intelligence community in anticipating the decline and collapse of the Soviet Union was generally good and sometimes outstanding. The intelligence community faced three basic tasks:

—First, analysts had to detect the overall slowdown of the Soviet economy and assess the underlying political, economic, and demographic factors that would make it difficult, if not impossible, for the Soviets to recover. This long-range analytical task had a time frame of approximately five to ten years, partly because that is the length of time such tidal socioeconomic changes require, and also because that encompasses several U.S. electoral cycles. This long-range warning gives elected officials time to reshape U.S. strategy and the electorate time to absorb and (perhaps) support it.

—Second, the intelligence community had to detect shorter-range trends that could plausibly lead to a crisis in Soviet politics and trigger collapse. Analysts had to postulate plausible scenarios and, as the Soviet Union drew closer to a crisis state, compare the probability of one scenario with another. This kind of warning, with a one-to-five-year time frame, permits a president to make significant adjustments during his term. The challenge here was partly one of imagination and partly one of understanding how to weigh the various political and economic factors that would determine the outcome.

—Third, the intelligence community had to warn U.S. officials when the Soviet collapse was imminent and the final endgame under way. The time frame for this task was a year or less. Analysts had to postulate specific "gates" that developments would need to pass through for the endgame to be triggered and then determine whether those gates had been passed.

Note that each task requires an increasing level of specificity and, by extension, that there were three opportunities in which U.S. intelligence analysts could fail. Note also that these levels of warning are interrelated. If analysts and officials are unaware of strategic changes in their adversary, they are less likely to succeed at tactical warning, and if they have failed the tactical problem, they will more likely be unprepared for the task of immediate warning.

Long-Range Warning

The challenge of anticipating the Soviet collapse was even greater for U.S. intelligence because the very notion of collapse was inconsistent with the thinking of most Western analysts and scholars. The prevailing view up to the late 1970s was that the Soviet Union would evolve, not collapse. It is true that some Sovietologists had long believed that a multiethnic, nondemocratic state dependent on a centrally planned economy was inherently unstable. Indeed, this was the assumption upon which containment was based.[3] But hardly any of these scholars were willing to hazard a time frame for a Soviet implosion. So their views were more of a theory than an intelligence estimate.

But by the mid-1970s there were growing signs that the Soviet economy and political system had ingrained, systemic problems. In the intelligence community, this economic slowdown was a basic underlying assumption for most intelligence analyses of the Soviet Union from the mid-1970s onward. Up to then, assessments often cited problems in the Soviet economy such as agricultural shortfalls and competition for resources and manufacturing capacity. After this point, it was generally understood that the Soviet Union as a whole was stagnating or declining economically, and that this slowdown would have profound political effects.

The main disagreement within the intelligence community was about how severe the effects of economic stagnation might be and how the Soviets would deal with them. The CIA and the Defense Intelligence Agency (DIA) took different approaches to measuring gross domestic product. In addition, while the CIA believed the economic slowdown might hinder the Soviet military buildup, the DIA believed that the continuing evidence of a military buildup illustrated that the Soviets were determined to outpace the United States despite economic constraints.

But hardly anyone in the intelligence community—especially the CIA—argued that the Soviets were in great shape, despite what some critics of the agency might suggest today. For example, in July 1977, the CIA reported the following:

> The Soviet economy faces serious strains in the decade ahead. The simple growth formula upon which the economy has relied for more than a generation—maximum inputs of labor and capital—will no longer yield the sizeable annual growth which has provided resources needed for competing claims. . . . Reduced growth, as is foreshadowed over the next decade, will make pursuit of these objectives much more difficult, and pose hard choices for the leadership, which can have a major impact on Soviet relations with Eastern Europe and the West.[4]

This assessment of a stagnating Soviet economy was, in turn, reflected in U.S. national strategy. Presidential Directive 18, which defined U.S. national strategy in the Carter administration, said that, "though successfully acquiring military power matching the United States, the Soviet Union continues to face major internal economic and national difficulties, and externally it has few genuinely committed allies while lately suffering setbacks in its relations with China, parts of Africa, and India."[5]

The Reagan administration went a step further by arguing that the United States could take advantage of these weaknesses and, through a planned, integrated strategy, accelerate the metamorphosis of the Communist regime. The resulting policy was a combination of economic pressure (through an arms race and trade sanctions) and political and military pressure (by supporting opponents of the Soviets and their allies in Eastern Europe, Latin America, and especially Afghanistan). According to National Security Decision Directive 32, U.S. goals were to "foster, if possible in concert with our allies, restraint in Soviet military spending, discourage Soviet adventurism, and weaken the

Soviet alliance system by forcing the USSR to bear the brunt of its economic shortcomings, and to encourage long-term liberalizing and nationalist tendencies within the Soviet Union and allied countries."[6]

In the late 1970s, though, before he became president, not even Ronald Reagan was willing to propose that the Soviet Union was on a course to collapse. In his speeches and essays during this period, Reagan was fully prepared to argue that the Soviet Union was evil and that its economy was inefficient and unable to sustain itself indefinitely. But he was not ready to say that it was on a course to collapse or that U.S. policy could accelerate this collapse. Reagan did not make those statements until after he entered office, specifically in his June 1982 address to the British Parliament, and his March 1983 speech to the National Association of Evangelicals.[7]

If the documentary record is clear, then why do so many people believe that the intelligence community failed to detect the Soviet Union's social and economic problems in the late 1970s?

One reason may have been that, at the time, the Soviet Union seemed ascendant. It had matched and even surpassed the United States in several measures of military capability, such as numbers of intercontinental ballistic missiles. It had expanded its influence through military cooperation treaties with clients in Asia, Africa, and the Middle East. The popular media (and the intelligence community) duly reported these events, and so the *zeitgeist* was that the Soviets were strong, and the United States was stuck in malaise. Since American officials did not effectively challenge this view in public, it was logical for Americans to conclude later that this reflected the intelligence they were reading.

Besides, there was nothing inevitable about Soviet collapse in the late 1970s. At that point many outcomes were possible. A more ruthless leader might have held the state together for another ten or fifteen years; witness Alexander Lukashenko in Belarus or Kim Jong-Il in North Korea. A more flexible leader might have managed a "soft landing" for the Soviet Communist Party; witness the current situation in China. It was impossible to provide a more definitive estimate fifteen years before the fact because the future was not yet certain. It never is.

Intermediate and Immediate Warning

By the early 1980s, the faltering Soviet economy was a given, the assumed context within which the intelligence community viewed Soviet political and military developments. For example, in 1985, as Mikhail Gorbachev took control, the National Intelligence Estimate on the Soviet domestic scene encapsulated the fundamental weaknesses in the Soviet state. It did not yet say that the conditions for collapse were present, but it explained how such a path was possible:

> The growth of the Soviet economy has been systematically decelerating since the 1950s as a consequence of dwindling supplies of new labor, the increasing cost of raw material inputs, and the constraints on factor productivity improvement imposed by the rigidities of the planning and management system. . . .
>
> The USSR is afflicted with a complex of domestic maladies that seriously worsened in the late 1970s and early 1980s. Their alleviation is one of the most significant and difficult challenges facing the Gorbachev regime. . . .
>
> Over the next five years, and for the foreseeable future, the troubles of the society will not present a challenge to the system of political control that guarantees Kremlin rule, nor will they threaten the economy with collapse. But, during the rest of the 1980s and well beyond, the domestic affairs of the USSR will be dominated by the efforts of the regime to grapple with these manifold problems. . . .
>
> Gorbachev has achieved an upswing in the mood of the Soviet elite and populace. But the prospects for his strategy over the next five years are mixed at best. . . .[8]

It is noteworthy that the forecasting horizon of the 1985 NIE was five years—normal for an NIE—and that the Soviet collapse occurred just beyond that horizon. It was still premature in 1985 for a definitive forecast. As the Soviet situation got progressively worse, so did the prognosis by the intelligence community. By spring 1989—more than two years before the attempted coup that led to the ultimate collapse of the regime—the intelligence community was telling U.S. leaders that the situation was essentially irretrievable and that a catastrophic end (from the Soviet leadership's point of view) was possible. The 1989 NIE said: "It will be very difficult for [Gorbachev] to achieve his goals. In the extreme, his policies and political power could be undermined and the political stability of the Soviet system could be fundamentally threatened. . . . [A]nxiety, fear, and anger [of the Soviet political elite] could still crystallize in an attempted coup, legal removal of Gorbachev, or even assassination."[9]

In April 1991 the Office of Soviet Analysis (SOVA), the office within the Directorate of Intelligence that followed developments in the USSR, told U.S. leaders explicitly that the Soviet Union was in a state of crisis, offered a poor prognosis, and spelled out specific scenarios in which the regime could implode. In a memo titled, "The Soviet Cauldron," the director of SOVA wrote,

> The economy is in a downward spiral with no end in sight . . . inflation was about 20 percent at the end of last year and will be at least double that this year . . . reliance on a top-down approach to problems, particularly in regard to republics, has generated a war of laws between various levels of power and created a legal mess to match the economic mess. . . . In this situation of growing chaos, explosive events have become increasingly possible.[10]

The memo then went on to describe possible outcomes, which included the assassination of Gorbachev or Boris Yeltsin, or a coup by "reactionary leaders who judge that the last chance to act had come"—which is, of course, exactly what later occurred.

Did the intelligence community provide immediate warning of the coup that triggered the final events of 1991? George Bush recalls in his memoirs:

> Besides the coup rumors in July, which Gorbachev had dismissed, there had been some recent indication that the hard-liners in Moscow might be up to something. On Saturday morning, August 17, Bob Gates had joined me at breakfast where we went over the Presidential Daily Briefing. In it was a report that the prospective signing of the Union treaty meant that time was running out for the hard-liners and they might feel compelled to act. Bob thought the threat was serious, although we had no specific information on what might happen or when. The next day the plotters struck.[11]

Robert Gates, then deputy national security adviser, and soon to become director of central intelligence, recalls the same briefing this way:

> CIA warned us at the White House that once the signing date [for the Union treaty] was set a deadline of sorts would be established for the conservatives to act. The changes that would follow signature, together with public sentiment, would make action after that date much more difficult. . . . [I]t fell to me on August 17 to hand the President his CIA *President's Daily Brief,* which warned of the strong chance that the conservatives would act within the next few days. It said, "The danger is growing that hardliners will precipitate large-scale violence," and described their efforts to prepare for an attempt to seize power. . . . [Bush] asked me if I thought the situation was serious and if the Agency's

> warning was valid. I explained the meaning of the August 20 signing ceremony, and said I thought he should take the PDB warning quite seriously.[12]

Note how Bush and Gates score this event differently, even though they basically agree on the facts. Gates believes he gave Bush warning because the CIA had previously established the prerequisite conditions for there to be a coup, and he says that the president's daily briefing for August 17 indicated that those conditions were present. Bush wanted to know whether any specific datum indicated what might happen or when, and Gates had no such specific datum.

These two different slants on the same material suggest just how controversial an assessment of whether one was "blindsided" can be, and they also highlight exactly where, if anywhere, the intelligence community fell short. To reach this last step in anticipating the Soviet collapse, the CIA would have needed first-hand information from the plotters themselves. Analysis alone can never fill that kind of gap, if only because at best an analysis is a probability assessment necessarily based on inference and deduction. The key datum that was lacking was, as Bush put, the "specific information on what might happen or when." This was a very tough piece of information to collect. Even Gorbachev lacked it, obviously.

The Persistent Myth—Why?

All in all, this is a good record. So why has the intelligence community's performance been so underappreciated, and why do officials to this day believe they were poorly served? What collective cognitive architecture explains the gap between the record and the perceptions, then and ever since?

One key reason is that the written record remained classified for several years after the Soviet Union disintegrated. Even when the most important documents, the National Intelligence Estimates, were declassified, they were initially not made widely available. The idea that the intelligence community was caught flat-footed took root by default because no one could point to specific documents that presented the intelligence community's consensus.

One example shows how such an information vacuum can be perpetuated into a "truth" with major effects. In 1991 former director of central intelligence Stansfield Turner published an article on the general topic of the future of intelligence. In one passage, Turner cited the apparent failure of the intelligence community to anticipate the Soviet collapse:

> We should not gloss over the enormity of this failure to forecast the magnitude of the Soviet crisis. We know now that there were many Soviet academics, economists and political thinkers, other than those officially presented to us by the Soviet government, who understood long before 1980 that the Soviet economic system was broken and that it was only a matter of time before someone had to try to repair it, as had Khrushchev. Yet I never heard a suggestion from the CIA, or the intelligence arms of the departments of defense or state, that numerous Soviets recognized a growing, systemic economic problem. . . . Today we hear some revisionist rumblings that the CIA did in fact see the Soviet collapse emerging after all. If some individual CIA analysts were more prescient than the corporate view, their ideas were filtered out in the bureaucratic process; and it is the corporate view that counts because that is what reaches the president and his advisers. On this one, the corporate view missed by a mile. . . . Why were so many of us so insensitive to the inevitable?[13]

This quotation has been repeated many times. It is usually portrayed as a mea culpa from a former head of the U.S. intelligence community, seemingly acknowledging that the community had failed to anticipate the Soviet collapse. However, it requires some parsing.

When Turner said he "never heard a suggestion" of a systemic weakness of the Soviet system, he was referring to the time he served as director of central intelligence, which was from 1977 to 1981. Also, when he criticized "revisionist rumblings" claiming the CIA did anticipate the collapse, neither the intelligence assessments reporting the Soviet decline in the 1980s nor the policy directives they supported had yet been released.

In reality, both the opinion of "individual CIA analysts" such as the director of SOVA and the "corporate view" expressed in NIEs concluded that the Soviet Union was in decline throughout the 1980s. These views were reaching the president and, as indicated earlier, were incorporated into presidential directives. But this paper trail was not made public until four years after Turner wrote. Indeed, the inherent problems and the decline of the Soviet economy had become the working assumption on which U.S. intelligence was based by the time Turner left office.

Nevertheless, this single quotation by Turner was cited repeatedly and written into the public record. Most notably, Senator Daniel Patrick Moynihan (D-N.Y.) referred to it during the confirmation hearing of Robert Gates to be director of central intelligence in 1991; included it in the 1996 report of the Commission on Protecting and Reducing Government Secrecy, which he chaired; cited it in a book he published in 1996; repeated it in an interview on *The NewsHour with Jim Lehrer* in 1998; mentioned it in his farewell speech to the U.S. Senate in 2002; and quoted it in his commencement address at Harvard in 2003. During this entire period, however, one is unable to find a single instance in which Moynihan quotes from an actual intelligence publication, such as those declassified in the early 1990s. Even when Moynihan submitted a bill in 1995 to abolish the CIA, he introduced his bill with a speech on the Senate floor that again claimed the intelligence community had failed to anticipate the Soviet collapse—and that again offered as its *only* evidence the aforementioned Turner quotation.[14] Despite its paucity of actual evidence, the impact of Moynihan's proposal was significant. It was (along with reaction to the Aldrich Ames espionage affair and concerns over the performance of intelligence in the first Gulf War) responsible for the establishment of the Aspin-Brown Commission and the contentious intelligence reforms of 1996.[15]

It is hard to square the documented record with Turner's comment from 1991. Perhaps Turner simply was unaware of the mainstream opinion of the intelligence community in the 1980s, after he left office. It is even more difficult to reconcile the views of anyone who did have access to intelligence and still believes the CIA and other agencies failed to provide warning. But this is precisely what the phenomenon of being blindsided is all about. The perception of being warned becomes separated from the reality of the warning that was provided. The best one can say is that this may be a problem more appropriately examined in the discipline of psychology, rather than in history or political science.

Those who criticize the intelligence community's assessment of the Soviet Union often get caught up in details, faulting it on specific findings that were secondary to the larger picture it was painting. In the early 1980s the CIA believed the Soviet gross domestic product was growing at about 2 percent annually. Today we know that its economic growth was essentially nonexistent. But the CIA was *not* trying to make the case that the Soviet Union was growing; as we have seen, the 2 percent growth estimate reflected a conclusion that, after remarkable growth in the 1950s and 1960s, the Soviet economy was grinding to a halt. The growth estimates were based on a modeling process that was controversial even at the time and should not divert attention from the key judgments that summarized the intelligence community's bedrock views—that the Soviet Union was in trouble.

Why Do Officials Feel Ill-Served?

One interesting feature about the controversies over the Soviet collapse is that some officials who had read the intelligence and understood full well what it said still believe they were, in some important sense, surprised when the end came. When Gorbachev was toppled, it seemed as though the Bush administration was not prepared to respond. Some critics wondered why the president had not moved earlier to embrace Yeltsin, who ultimately prevailed. Would better intelligence have made a difference?

As we have seen, President Bush described the warning presented to him as too limited for taking action. But his diary entry on August 19, 1991, suggests that more factors were in play than just this intelligence report. Reflecting on the day's events, Bush wrote:

> [T]he questions for the most part were okay; [such as] "Why were you surprised." There will be a lot of talking heads analyzing the policy, but in my view this *totally* vindicates our policy of trying to stay with Gorbachev. If we had pulled the rug out from under Gorbachev and swung toward Yeltsin you'd have seen a military crackdown far in excess of the ugliness that's taking place now. I'm convinced of that. I think what we must do is see that the progress made under Gorbachev is not turned around.[16]

In other words, the Bush administration—despite receiving and acknowledging that conditions were ripe for a coup—believed it had no option other than to stick with Gorbachev. This was a judgment based less on intelligence information or the lack thereof than on the administration's policy objectives. The administration's goals were established by National Security Directive 23, which Bush signed on September 22, 1989:

> Our policy is not designed to help a particular leader or set of leaders in the Soviet Union. We seek, instead, fundamental alterations in Soviet military force structure, institutions, and practices which can only be reversed at great cost, economically and politically, to the Soviet Union. If we succeed, the ground for cooperation will widen, while that for conflict narrows. The U.S.-Soviet relationship may still be fundamentally competitive, but it will be less militarized and safer. . . . U.S. policy will encourage fundamental political and economic reform, including freely contested elections, in East-Central Europe, so that states in that region may once again be productive members of a prosperous, peaceful, and democratic Europe, whole and free of fear of Soviet intervention.[17]

In short, the Bush administration did *not* intend to destabilize the Soviet Union (though it did envision the breakup of the Warsaw Pact). This is a subtle but significant difference from the policy of the Reagan administration, which, as shown, said that the United States would seek to exploit fissures within the Warsaw Pact and the weakness of the Soviet economy. The Bush administration, in contrast, aimed to use economic pressure as a means to encourage the existing regime to moderate. National Security Directive 23 said:

> The purpose of our forces is not to put pressure on a weak Soviet economy or to seek military superiority. Rather, U.S. policy recognizes the need to provide a hedge against uncertain long-term developments in the Soviet Union and to impress upon the Soviet leadership the wisdom of pursuing a responsible course. . . . Where possible, the United States should promote Western values and ideas within the Soviet Union, not in the spirit of provocation or destabilization, but as a means to lay a firm foundation for a cooperative relationship.

Note that the directive says, "impress upon the *Soviet* leadership [emphasis added]"—meaning that the U.S. leadership expected the Soviet regime to remain in place as the directive was implemented. The Reagan administration's view was different, as expressed in Reagan's address to the British Parliament on June 8, 1982:

> I have discussed on other occasions . . . the elements of Western policies toward the Soviet Union to safeguard our interests and protect the peace. What I am describing now is a plan and a hope for the long term—the march of freedom and democracy which will leave Marxism-Leninism on the ash-heap of history as it has left other tyrannies which stifle the freedom and muzzle the self-expression of the people.[18]

In other words, the Reagan administration might not have sought the collapse of the Soviet regime, but it envisioned that regime would fall and thus would have been less surprised by the collapse. Also, it is significant that the Reagan policy was adopted before Gorbachev rose to power and provided, in the words of Margaret Thatcher, someone with whom "we can do business." Had there been a third Reagan administration, it might have come to resemble the Bush administration as it adjusted to changes in Soviet realities.

In any event, the Bush policy was predicated on continuing to deal with the Soviet regime. So when the regime collapsed, there was, as Bush recalled, a natural tendency for observers to ask if the administration had been caught unaware. Apparently it was, but if it was, that was not because of an intelligence failure but rather the result of an intentional decision to support Gorbachev to the end.

The Real Thing

Americans *know* what an actual intelligence failure looks like. Recall, for example, the August 1978 assessment by the CIA that "Iran is not in a revolutionary or even a pre-revolutionary state," six months before the shah fell.[19] Or more recently, the October 2002 NIE, which said that, "in the view of most agencies, Baghdad is reconstituting its nuclear weapons program."[20] These are the kinds of statements analysts lose sleep over because, despite the cliché about coordinated intelligence reflecting the lowest common denominator, one of the hallmarks of American intelligence analysis is the constant pressure to publish clear, definitive statements. So when the analysis is wrong, it is apt to be clearly wrong.

Conversely, when it is correct, it is clearly correct. Only the most convoluted reasoning can turn the summaries and key judgments of the intelligence community's analysis of the Soviet Union in the 1980s into a case that the intelligence community "missed" the Soviet collapse.

Holding intelligence organizations accountable for their performance is important. But acknowledging when intelligence is successful is equally important. So too is appreciating the differences between an intelligence failure and policy frailties whose sources lie elsewhere. Without an understanding that such things can happen, we are certain to be blindsided in the future.

5 *Econoshocks: The East Asian Crisis Case*

David Hale

The East Asian financial crisis of 1997–98 was one of the most dramatic economic events of the twentieth century. A region that had enjoyed several years of robust economic growth was suddenly plunged into a financial crisis that produced widespread bankruptcies and sharply higher unemployment. The crisis brought down one of Asia's oldest dictators, Indonesia's Suharto, and helped to topple a democratically elected government in Thailand. It forced the International Monetary Fund to play a leadership role in organizing rescue programs but also brought the IMF severe criticism for imposing fiscal austerity on countries that had already fallen into recession. It set the stage for new experiments in regional financial cooperation that persist today and that could ultimately evolve into the creation of new institutions for promoting both free trade and monetary union. But the financial crisis also created conditions for today's imbalanced global payments situation, in which savings are flowing upstream from developing countries to developed ones, mainly the United States. The effects of the 1997–98 crisis have thus yet to fully play out.

Before the Storm

The East Asian crisis took most people by surprise because the region had a history of superior economic performance. Many countries had enjoyed output growth in the 5–7 percent range for several years. Some countries had also enjoyed great stock market booms for several years. From 1975 to the end of

1994, the South Korean stock market index had risen 1,604 percent; that of Malaysia, 1,733 percent; and Thailand, 1,711 percent. Immediately before the crisis, there were large capital inflows to the region that grew from $21 billion during 1992 to $64 billion during 1996. The IMF issued positive reports on Asia during the mid-1990s and, at a major conference in Jakarta in late 1996, concluded that the outlook for ASEAN (Association of Southeast Asian Nations) was still bright. Since many of the private economists who followed East Asia for the major investment banks had previously worked for the IMF, they tended to reinforce the consensus view that growth would remain robust indefinitely.

A variety of factors helped set the stage for the crisis. Their importance varied by country, but the central unifying theme was the role of confidence itself. East Asia had emerged by the mid-1990s as a region with large current account deficits and thus a need for large, offsetting capital inflows. When confidence is robust, it is easy to attract capital. But large capital inflows often encourage speculative behavior, such as excessive real estate development, which can trigger banking and other problems. When investors lose confidence because of signs of deterioration in the quality of bank assets, capital flows tend to reverse themselves and trigger currency devaluations, which in turn can lead to financial crises. This is exactly what happened in most East and Southeast Asian countries in 1997–98.

A few commentaries in the years before the crisis did question the sustainability of the East Asian development model. For example, Paul Krugman suggested in 1994 that the East Asian boom was a by-product of excessive investment rather than high-productivity growth and that it therefore was not sustainable.[1] Krugman riled Asian policymakers by pointing out that rapid growth in the Soviet Union had also been based on high levels of investment spending. Other economists, however, contended that Krugman's claims were too stark. They acknowledged that East Asia had a high level of investment spending, but they felt that productivity was contributing to growth as well. They also argued that East Asian investment had been based on market criteria, not bureaucratic fiat, and pointed to a much higher rate of return on East Asian investment than had ever existed in the former Soviet Union.

Jim Walker of Credit Lyonnais Securities Asia also published a report in December 1994 comparing postdevaluation Mexico to Asia.[2] Walker saw some similarities at play and was more skeptical than most about the future of the Asia growth story. But even he argued that Asia looked much safer than Latin America.

A more distressing report appeared about eighteen months later, in June 1996, from SBC Warburg about declining profitability in East Asia.[3] The report examined how Japan had been able to boost export growth and profitability for many years through an undervalued currency but noted that the currency markets were no longer as supportive of Asian exports and profitability as they had been previously. The report therefore warned "that countries are far less able to resist real exchange rate appreciation pressures than they were even a decade ago" and that "the corporate profit share in GNP [gross national product] is probably falling and could further hamper the ability of the corporate sector to deliver profit growth in line with economic growth."

The Warburg report, influential among fund managers, was soon followed by a United Nations report warning that the benign first stage of industrial takeoff in East Asia was coming to an end and that new challenges in sustaining large current account deficits would lie ahead.[4] The report noted that "the second-tier NIEs [newly industrial economies] may be unable to sustain large current-account deficits over the longer term; they need to reduce their trade deficits so as to minimize the risk of serious balance of payments problems and sharp slowdown in growth."

Concerns about the Asian economies in the Warburg and UN reports focused on long-term structural issues. A deterioration in East Asian exports during 1996 gave some confirmation of these risks. Thailand's exports fell by 1 percent during 1996 after increasing by 25 percent during 1995. Malaysia's export growth slowed to 6 percent from 26 percent. South Korea's export growth fell from 30 percent to 4 percent. Indonesia's growth rate eased to 10 percent from 13 percent. Thailand clearly faced potential competitiveness problems because its real wage growth had accelerated to 9 percent during 1990–94 from 2 percent previously. But most observers concluded that the primary problem for the region was nothing long term or structural but rather a slowdown in the global electronics industry that had emerged as an important export market for many countries.

As it happened, the export slowdown was not the primary cause of financial crisis that first hit Thailand in 1997, nor was it longer-term productivity issues about which the Warburg and UN reports had warned. The crisis was the result of a totally different factor: leverage. Thailand had established an international banking facility during the early 1990s to attract global bank lending. This facility allowed Thai banks and financial institutions to make dollar loans to their local customers. Thai companies preferred borrowing in dollars because the interest rates were several hundred basis points below the cost of loans denominated in Thai bahts. As a consequence of the new bank facility, Thai external borrowing grew from $40 billion in 1992 to $80 billion in March 1997. Total outstanding debt grew from 34 percent of GDP (gross domestic product) in 1990 to 51 percent in 1996, an increase generated almost entirely by the private sector. Almost 36 percent of the debt was short term, scheduled to mature in fewer than twelve months.

In August 1997, the Bank of Thailand revealed that its foreign debt stood at about $90 billion, of which $73 billion consisted of loans to private companies—with $20 billion falling due by year end. A large share of the borrowing had been used to finance property development. Between 1992 and 1996, 755,000 housing units were built in Bangkok, twice the number estimated in the Thai national plan. By 1997 Thailand had a residential vacancy rate of 25–30 percent and a commercial vacancy rate of 14 percent, with many large buildings still awaiting completion. The lending boom created two interwoven forms of vulnerability for the Thai private sector. First, the overinvestment in real estate created credit-quality risks. Second, many borrowers had financed their activities in dollars and thus faced a currency risk if the Thai baht were devalued. But investors were not particularly worried about this. Thailand had a history of financial crises, but none had led to a major economic meltdown. In 1983–85, for example, a crisis led to a government bailout of the banks and a 25 percent devaluation of the baht. But the instability had stopped there. What investors did not see in 1997 was the connection between the banking problems and the dollar leveraging. In 1983–85, devaluation did not set the stage for a wave of bankruptcies, so before the crisis hit in 1997 this remained the expectation of most observers.

In retrospect, the analysis that came closest to predicting the *dynamics* of the East Asian crisis was a March 1996 U.S. Federal Reserve report by Carmen Reinhart and Graciela Kaminsky on banking crises and balance-of-payment problems.[5] The paper examined the history of financial crises in several countries, looking specifically at the link between banking problems and the exchange rate. After reviewing the experience of several countries, Reinhart and Kaminsky found a pattern in which countries deregulated their financial systems and experienced a surge of lending that produced credit-quality problems. The bank problems would constrain the ability of central banks to tighten monetary policy and thus set the stage for currency depreciation. They found that such crises tended to be more severe in developing countries than in industrial ones. One of the best examples of such a crisis was Chile in 1983, but they found similar examples in Argentina (1981), Brazil (1987), Colombia (1983), Finland (1983), Mexico (1994), Peru (1985), and Turkey (1984).

Despite this evidence, on the eve of the East Asian financial crisis few believed that the region was vulnerable to major financial shocks. East Asian countries, after all, had but modest budget deficits and generally low inflation. The Reinhart-Kaminsky paper therefore did not produce much discussion in East Asia because most of the crises they reviewed had been in Latin America, and East Asia was free of Latin America's problems with large fiscal deficits. There was not much focus in East Asia on the issue of private sector debt either, despite the large increases that had occurred in corporate and household leverage in Thailand, Malaysia, and Indonesia during the first half of the 1990s. That was because private sector debt had not been identified as a major factor in earlier crises.

Two other factors also helped to boost banker confidence in the East Asian countries despite the rapid growth of leverage. First, bankers perceived a close link between governments and business that they believed would lessen the risk that banks or private companies would go bankrupt. The data on the concentration of share ownership in various Asian countries illustrated the power of family groups. The share of stock market capitalization controlled by the top fifteen families was 62 percent in Indonesia, 38 percent in Korea, 28 percent in Malaysia, and 53 percent in Thailand. The banking system was also highly concentrated. The market share of the five leading banking institutions was 41 percent in Indonesia, 75 percent in Korea, 41 percent in Malaysia, and 70 percent in Thailand. The political links between business and government added a clear—but unrecognized—moral hazard dimension to the East Asian lending boom.

Second, investors were confident that Japan would play a supporting role in the event of any financial problems because of its large investments and bank loans in the region. Japanese banks had 99 offices in East Asia during 1980, 313 in 1990, and 363 in 1994. In 1991, 19 percent of all Japanese international bank lending went to East Asia; in 1994, the share had risen to 26 percent. Japanese banks held 37 percent of East Asia's external bank liabilities. Japan also provided $10 billion in loans to China, a sum equal to 75 percent of China's total bilateral borrowing.

As a result of the strong yen, Japanese companies also placed a great deal of foreign direct investment (FDI) in East Asia. Between 1992 and 1995 East Asia took one-fourth of Japan's total FDI, or $35 billion. Almost 60 percent of this FDI was in manufacturing as Japanese auto and electronics companies sought to reduce their costs to remain competitive. The problem with Japan's role was that its banks faced a major problem with nonperforming loans at home. These banks became much more cautious after 1996, thus contributing to the sudden sharp reduction of lending to the region. Japan recognized the severity of the crisis during the autumn of 1997, and its vice minister of finance, Eisuke Sakakibara, proposed the creation of a regional IMF to help provide liquidity for troubled countries. But the idea was promptly rejected by the U.S. government and received no support from China either.

In sum, on the eve of the crisis, some analysts had spotted weaknesses and reported them, generating some useful and interesting debates. In the case of the Sakakibara proposal, some officials even proposed protective actions. But overall, confidence prevailed—and the crisis hit anyway.

Damage Done, Lessons Learned

This is not the place to review exactly how the crisis emerged, proceeded, spread, and deepened. Suffice it to say that many factors came into play: currency speculators caused a good deal of trouble but were able to do so only because some currencies were deliberately undervalued for the purpose of spurring exports, and some economies were overleveraged in dollar lending amid frailties in newly liberalized financial sectors. The consequences of the crisis were devastating. The East Asian recession during 1998 was the most severe in modern history. Real GDP fell by 13.1 percent in Indonesia, 10.5 percent in Thailand, 7.4 percent in Malaysia, and 0.6 percent in Philippines. Singapore also suffered a contraction of 0.9 percent of GDP even though it did not experience a banking crisis. Investment fell by 44.3 percent in Thailand, 44.0 percent in Malaysia, 33.0 percent in Indonesia, and 11.2 percent in the Philippines. Consumption also declined because of job losses and the collapse in credit availability—by 11.5 percent in Thailand, 10.2 percent in Malaysia, 6.2 percent in Indonesia, and 3.4 percent in Singapore.

The large currency declines improved the competitive position of most Asian countries, but export growth did not rebound quickly in most cases. In 1998 exports grew by 8.2 percent in Thailand, 11.2 percent in Indonesia, and 0.5 percent in Malaysia. In 1999 exports rebounded by 13.2 percent in Malaysia, 10.6 percent in Singapore, and 9.0 percent in Thailand, but they fell by 31.8 percent in Indonesia because companies in that country no longer had access to trade finance. There was no rebound in Indonesian trade until 2000. Severe recession also turned the region from a major capital importer into a capital exporter. In the aftermath of the crisis, massive current account surpluses developed. Thailand's averaged 12.8 percent of GDP in 1998 and 10.2 percent in 1999. Malaysia's current account surplus averaged 13.2 percent of GDP in 1998 and 15.9 percent in 1999. Singapore's surplus shot up to 22.2 percent of GDP in 1998 and 17.9 percent in 1999. The Philippines had a surplus of 2.0 percent of GDP in 1998 and 9.5 percent in 1999. Indonesia had a surplus of 4.2 percent of GDP in 1998 and 4.1 percent in 1999.

The major lesson from the East Asian crisis is that financial markets, newly liberalized ones in particular, often operate with incomplete information and thus can allocate resources inefficiently. East Asian countries enjoyed a high level of investor confidence because they had produced superior returns over a period of many years. High confidence led to overleveraging and speculative investments in real estate that proved to be unprofitable. When investors discovered that the boom was at risk, they panicked and withdrew capital. The loss of funding led to a collapse in currencies and a wave of bankruptcies in the private sector among companies with foreign currency leverage. Despite different initial conditions in each country, the crisis evinced a recurring pattern—prolonged periods of currency stability, newly deregulated financial systems, large amounts of short maturity debt, high levels of dollar leverage, and central banks constrained by debt.

The reason so many people were surprised is that no one put together the various pieces at one time. Analysts had paid attention to different dimensions of the region's vulnerability. Krugman focused on high investment rates but not leverage. The UN was concerned about upward pressure on real wages and labor shortages but little else. Many were concerned about the weakness of exports during 1996 because of a slowdown in the global electronics industry. In early 1997 Thailand's bank stock analysts realized their sector had major credit-quality problems and warned global investors to avoid the shares. Many sold their Thai equity positions, and the Soros organization, in particular, engaged in massive short sale of the baht. No one connected all the dots, however, to see where such behavior would lead.

The greatest surprise of all, perhaps, was how little the IMF knew about the potential bank asset quality and leverage problems in the private sector. IMF analysts had been so focused on government deficits and monetary policy that they neglected the issue of private sector financial conditions. IMF officials had lunch with central bank governors. They did not meet the entrepreneurs borrowing billions of dollars from global banks to finance real estate projects (Thailand and Malaysia) or steel mills (Korea). Rather like the proverbial generals always fighting the last war, IMF officials were keen to see signs of the last spate of crises and missed the signs of a different kind of crisis right under their noses.

Downstream Effects: New Problem, New Surprises

East Asia did not abandon market economics or capitalism despite the large increases in unemployment and poverty after 1997. On the contrary, the IMF programs forced countries to pursue microeconomic reforms that opened the door to more engagement with the global economy, including reduced trade protection and expanded opportunities for foreign direct investment. As a result, East Asia enjoyed a sustained recovery after 1999 and was able to restore the health of its domestic financial system. The country that experienced the largest devaluation and the greatest banking crisis, Indonesia, has been able to reduce its government debt from 92 percent of GDP in 2000 to 46 percent currently.

The crisis had produced other significant side effects, some, as suggested earlier, with profound consequences for the current balance-of-payments equilibrium of the world economy. After the crisis, the investment ratios of East Asia never fully recovered. Except for China and Vietnam, investment ratios in most East Asian countries are still 5–10 percent below their levels of the early 1990s. East Asian corporate sectors have been so conservative since 1998 that debt-equity ratios have fallen from 80 percent to 20 percent. As a result, most East Asian countries are running current account surpluses and have built up large foreign exchange reserves. The region as a whole, including Japan, has reserves of $2.7 trillion, about two-thirds of the global total. These reserves are invested overwhelmingly in U.S. government securities, making it possible for the Bush administration to run large fiscal deficits while the U.S. economy enjoys the benefits of low bond yields and rapidly increasing house prices. The American equity market boom of 1999–2000 and the American housing boom of 2002–06 are therefore in part a consequence of the East Asian financial crisis. That, too, has to rank as a surprise.

Surprised or not, the U.S. Congress has not been especially grateful for this help from East Asia. It has criticized East Asian countries, especially China, for deliberately undervaluing their currencies to boost exports, the result being a large U.S. trade deficit. Congress seems not to understand how the 1997–98 crisis depressed investment in most of Asia. China, by contrast, has been having one of the greatest capital spending booms in recorded history, with investment share of GDP at 48 percent during 2006, compared with 40–41 percent in Southeast Asia and Korea during the mid-1990s. But this has not produced a current account deficit because China also has the highest savings rate in the world. China can fund a capital spending boom with domestic resources, but it is still enjoying the benefit of $55 billion a year of foreign direct investment. It is foreign firms that have turned China into an export powerhouse by producing almost 60 percent of the country's foreign trade.

Some economists contend that the world has returned de facto to a Bretton Woods fixed exchange rate system in the Asia-Pacific region because of the complementary nature of East Asia's surplus savings and America's savings deficit. These economists believe the new equilibrium can be sustained indefinitely because East Asian central banks will intervene in the market to support the U.S. dollar when private capital flows slow down. And indeed, Japan and China intervened massively to support the dollar during 2003 and 2004. But since then only China has been intervening to maintain a stable currency. No official intervention from Japan has been necessary because Japanese private investors have been exporting massive amounts of capital in search of higher interest rates than Japan can offer.

There is no way to predict exactly how long the global payments equilibrium can continue. Because China derives 10 percent of its GDP from exports to America, it is doubtful that Beijing will allow its currency to appreciate dramatically against the U.S. dollar. The Japanese economy is now experiencing a healthy upturn after many years of recession, so Japan might be more willing to tolerate a strong yen. Exports to America are only 2.9 percent of Japan's GDP. At this point only one thing is certain: Americans have become very complacent about their budget deficits and housing inflation because of the country's ease at importing capital. Few regard the large account deficit as a threat. They view it instead as a proxy for the world's enthusiasm about investing in the United States.

But the United States today appears to be more vulnerable to a balance-of-payments crisis than East Asia was a decade ago. It has a large current account deficit because of a government budget deficit and a lack of private savings. East Asia had large current account deficits because of a high level of private investment. The U.S. dollar is less vulnerable to a crisis than East Asian currencies were in the mid-1990s because of the dollar's global role as a reserve currency and the large size of America's asset markets. The current account deficit is large in relation to GDP (7 percent), but it is not large in relation to America's asset markets. The household sector has assets of $64 trillion, and the nonfinancial business sector has assets of $32 trillion. If debt is subtracted, the net value of private assets is about $70 trillion. The current account deficit is therefore equal to only 1 percent of private assets, so dollar optimists are confident there are no fundamental obstacles to funding the U.S. external deficit.

Foreign investors already own large shares of some U.S. asset markets: 47 percent of the market for Treasury securities ($2.27 trillion), 29.5 percent of the market for corporate bonds ($2.52 trillion), 15.1 percent of the equity market ($2.85 trillion), and 14.9 percent of the market for agency debt ($951 billion). These ratios imply that $30 trillion of liquid securities is still available for foreign investors to purchase. American asset markets also have been expanding at an annual rate of 8–9 percent, so no shortfall of securities for foreign investors to purchase is likely. The large holdings of Treasury securities are concentrated in the foreign exchange reserves of East Asian central banks trying to resist sharp appreciation of their exchange rates against the dollar. If they continue to purchase $300 billion-$400 billion of Treasury debt, the United States may have to expand its budget deficit to prevent their share from rising above 60 percent.

There is a risk, too, that the dollar could decline over the next twelve to eighteen months because of the American economy's slowing. The United States has enjoyed robust consumption growth since 2002 because of steadily rising house prices. Households have been able to borrow against rising house prices to finance consumption. The property market is now cooling and house prices are starting to decline in some overheated cities such as Miami and Las Vegas. The slump in consumption could depress output growth to only 2.5 percent during 2007 from 4–5 percent recently. In such a scenario, demand for the dollar could fade because of falling money market yields and a squeeze on corporate profit margins depressing the equity market. But the U.S. economy will need a slowdown merely to stabilize the current account deficit because it has a potential shortage of manufacturing capacity. If the current account deficit were to decline by 25 percent, the U.S. capacity utilization rate would rise to 88 percent from 82 percent, a level the Federal Reserve would regard as dangerously inflationary. The Fed would want to reinforce the slowdown in domestic spending to create surplus capacity for reducing the current account deficit.

Into the Uncertain Future

Economic analysts can sound fairly confident about their predictions. It is prudent to sound confident about what one is paid to do. But the global financial environment is totally different today from what it was during the mid-1990s. In that period, the developing countries ran a current account deficit of more than $100 billion. In 2005 they ran a current account surplus exceeding $400 billion. The East Asian financial crisis turned countries that had been large capital importers into capital exporters. Today, only a few developing and mid-range countries are running current account deficits (Greece, Hungary, Iceland, India, Poland, South Africa, and Turkey). The biggest deficit now belongs to the United States, which has been importing capital on a large scale from East Asia as well as from the oil-producing countries that are benefiting from high oil prices. East Asia had a crisis in 1997–98 because its boom encouraged a misallocation of capital to sectors such as property in Thailand and heavy industry in Korea. It was the misuse of capital rather than existence of deficits that provoked a loss of confidence, capital flight, and a collapse of regional currencies. It could be argued that the United States is now also misallocating capital to consumption and housing, but the markets are indifferent to these concerns because of the scale of America's asset markets. What, exactly, could go massively wrong the next time? I wish I knew. That is a surprise everyone would like to avoid.

The East Asian crisis will continue to have a special place in the history of financial disasters. It resulted from traditional excesses that were not correctly perceived until they reached an alarming size. Local authorities inadequately regulated the banks, and international organizations such as the IMF poorly monitored systemic risk. The experience was so searing that neither the East Asian countries nor the IMF will soon forget what happened. East Asia is also sitting on an immense stock of foreign exchange reserves to lessen the risk that it will ever again experience a liquidity shock. The developing countries are currently enjoying good growth rates because of high commodity prices and low interest rates in the old industrial countries. They are enjoying the benefits of positive terms of trade and low borrowing costs. The strongest currency in the world during 2005 was the Zambian kwacha, which appreciated by 27 percent against the U.S. dollar because robust copper prices produced an influx of foreign capital to Zambia. If the United States and China experience a major economic slowdown, commodity prices will decline and dampen the growth rates of countries such as Zambia. But because everyone expects commodity prices to be cyclical, it is doubtful that a major crisis would ensue. There can be a major crisis only if investors and bankers experience a major surprise and discover risks that were unanticipated. The magnitude of the booms now occurring in China and India suggests that they could be candidates for a crisis, but as they learned many lessons from East Asia's experience during 1997–98, it is doubtful that they will allow the markets to create the same systemic vulnerabilities that struck Thailand, Korea, and Indonesia. China has made tremendous strides during the past three years in strengthening its insolvent banking system. Two of the large state-owned banks have listed shares on the Hong Kong stock exchange and raised over $20 billion of new capital. Their market capitalizations also exceed $100 billion and thus place them among the world's top ten banks. China is also running a current account surplus of 6 percent of GDP and will soon have over $1 trillion in foreign exchange reserves. China has many unresolved economic problems, but it does not manifest the preconditions for an East Asia–style liquidity crisis.

The most likely candidates for crisis will continue to be countries that trust markets to allocate capital efficiently and allow global investors the freedom to transfer funds in and out of their asset markets easily. The markets could also be vulnerable to Japanese monetary tightening in the future because hedge funds have borrowed large sums in yen to invest in higher-yielding emerging market securities. The prospect that further monetary tightening will reduce the world's surplus liquidity could produce a correction in asset markets all over the world during the year ahead, but the preconditions for a major crisis do not exist because of the legacy of the East Asian events of 1997–98. Despite the buoyant world economy since 2003, there has been no rush to overleverage companies in developing countries with dollar debt and no surge of property development in emerging financial centers.

Indeed, the great real estate inflation since 2000 has been in Australia, Britain, New Zealand, South Africa, Spain, and the United States. It is clear there have been more excesses in the old industrial countries during the past five years than in the developing countries, so the next major shocks to the global financial system are more likely to come from North America, Europe, and Japan than from other East Asian countries or Latin America. It will probably take another generation for bankers to forget about the East Asian financial crisis and be prepared to promote high-risk forms of leverage in the developing countries. The final legacy of the events of 1997–98 will thus be several more years of financial caution producing current account surpluses and excess liquidity in East Asia for recycling back to the highly leveraged consumers of North America, Australia, and other English-speaking countries. Then again, we could be surprised once more.

Part II

Cases: Looking Ahead

6

The Once and Future DARPA

William B. Bonvillian

The idea that technological innovation can be a driver of both winning armies and growing economies is at least as old as the Appian Way. A transportation network very sophisticated for its time, the Appian Way was an accelerator for Roman military prowess and commerce. It allowed Romans to move armies quickly and with better command and control, and it facilitated commerce—fueling a growing economy that sustained the republic and later the empire. It was, literally, an early information superhighway.

For nearly the next two millennia the example of the Appian Way inspired imitation. Libraries are full of books that discuss the history of science and technology, and virtually all of them have one thing in common: the conviction that innovation matters, sometimes decisively, in the economic, social, military, and political affairs of mankind.

True enough, but something important happened on the way to the twenty-first century. Even as military technology grew in lethality, it was still very rarely decisive in military or political outcomes. In theory at least, Julius Caesar and George Patton could have sat discussing tactics for desert warfare or crossing the Rhine and understood one another tolerably well. Weapons mattered, but not necessarily more than soldiers' skill, morale, leadership, planning, training, weather, and luck. That began to change during World War II, when it first became apparent that new technology by itself—not just more sophisticated implements in the hands of competent soldiers—could win wars. The foremost examples were microwave radar and proximity fuse advances, which emerged from the Radiation Laboratory at the Massachusetts Institute of Technology, and, of course, the atom bomb from Los Alamos. These were war-*winning* technologies in which applied science had reached a stage where it could transform war, and geopolitics with it, in ways heretofore barely imaginable.

The evolution of late-twentieth-century military technology was part of a much bigger picture of innovation transformation. Carlotta Perez has argued persuasively that, starting with the onset of the Industrial Revolution in Britain in 1770, an industrial transformation has occurred roughly every half century.[1] Technology-based innovation cycles have flowed out in long, multidecadal waves, transforming economies and the way societies organize around them. Military innovation and power has spun out from these waves in such a way that world military leadership has tended to parallel leadership in technological innovation.

The United States has led the last three innovation cycles, with information technology at the epicenter of the latest wave. As with the Appian Way, the core techniques of the current innovation wave generate mutually reinforcing economic and military advantages. The obvious insight here is that the relative power of political entities has a great deal to do with technological leadership. What is less obvious is that military applications of technological innovation are rarely direct and cannot be sustained in isolation from technological change in society as a whole.

What is also not obvious is that the relative importance of military technology to national power is not constant. The United States today is without question the strongest military power and the wealthiest society on earth. But even with its immense military power, the U.S. government arguably cannot achieve political ends comparable to those achieved by the Wilson administration in 1917–18. In matters regarding applications of core scientific-technological innovation to U.S. national power today, Americans clearly do not wish to fall behind others in military sophistication. Force is still the *ultima ratio* in the political affairs of the human species, like it or not. But it does not follow that the application of cutting-edge innovation to the military arts is the *only* domain that should concern government.

It does not take a rocket scientist, as the aphorism goes, to realize that the United States, its allies, and the world at large have a potentially serious energy problem. Economic power is the heart of American "soft" power and the backbone of its military power; energy has become an Achilles' heel to both. The record shows that every presidential administration since that of Richard Nixon not only has acknowledged the problem and understood its broader geopolitical implications but has pledged to actually do something about it. All of them have failed. The history of U.S. energy policy over the past three decades, under Republican and Democratic stewardship alike, is one of the saddest stories in American political history. For more than thirty years it has been understood that science and technology would ultimately provide the basis for a solution to the energy dilemma, yet the innovation paradigm that keeps the U.S. military the most sophisticated in the world has not been applied to the energy sector.

That paradigm can be summed up in a single beltway-savvy acronym: DARPA (the Defense Advanced Research Projects Agency). A question American political leaders should be asking, but mostly are not—especially within the current, sometimes science-challenged administration—is how the DARPA model can be cloned and applied to the energy dilemma. When politicians occasionally make speeches calling for a "Manhattan Project for energy," they are actually onto something—or barely clinging, at least, to the edge of a thought. But few such speechmakers have the slightest idea how the Manhattan Project was created and why it succeeded.

Thanks in significant part to DARPA's lessons, a fair bit is known about the causal factors behind innovation and its successful application. Growth economics teaches that innovation yields growth through two direct innovation factors: state-of-the-art research and development, and the talent behind that R&D. I posit here a third factor, which involves not science as such or the fabrication of the hardware derived from it, but rather the institutional setup in which research facilities and human talent best combine. The deliberate creation of the nexus where science and technology is best organized is called "innovation organization." Innovation organization in turn operates at two interwoven levels: personal and institutional. At the personal level, innovation differs from scientific discovery or invention. Solo operators can produce discovery, but innovation is team-and-network-intensive.[2] Systemic innovation requires linking scientific discovery to technological invention and then multiplying applications of breakthrough inventions to create sharp productivity gains with the potential to transform significant segments of an economy. This activity requires deep institutional connections between the "R" and the "D" stages.

The DARPA model, if its innovation organization lessons are understood and applied, has the potential to transform energy technology dramatically. If U.S. power in this century falls victim to the multiple implications of a global energy situation run deeply amok, Americans and their political leaders will have no one but themselves to blame. It is therefore necessary to understand the history and nature of DARPA, distill out its optimal innovation system, and set up as quickly as possible a new innovation system aimed at a range of energy technologies.

Science, Connected and Pipelined

The precursors of U.S. government science and technology organization go back to the Lincoln administration, when the National Academy of Sciences was created. But for my purposes the relevant history dates from World War II and comes from a kind of Dr. Dolittle "Pushmi-Pullyu" relationship between civilian economic and defense sectors. Acting as President Franklin D. Roosevelt's personal science executive during the war, Dr. Vannevar Bush led this charge. He was allied with a remarkable group of fellow science organizers, including investment banker and scientist Alfred Loomis, Berkeley physicist Ernest Lawrence, and two university presidents, James Conant of Harvard and Karl Compton of MIT.

Loomis was a particularly interesting and critical character in all this. He loved science, but family needs compelled him to become lawyer.[3] Loomis nevertheless found a way to combine his science and legal skills to become a leading Wall Street financier for the emerging electric utility industry in the 1920s. Anticipating the market crash, Loomis cashed out in 1928 with his great fortune intact, which he then used to set up a private lab at his Tuxedo Park, New York, estate. There in the 1930s, Loomis assembled a "who's who" of prewar physicists. Loomis's personal obsession was microwave physics, but his organizational talents were also evident. So as World War II loomed, Vannevar Bush asked Loomis to join Roosevelt's National Defense Research Council to mobilize scientists for the war effort.

At about this point, one of those inexplicably satyrish moments in history jumped forth. The U.S. military expressed no interest in Britain's work on microwave radar, for fear of having to trade U.S. secrets to obtain it. To rescue America from its own shortsightedness, one night in 1940 Loomis took a delegation, dispatched by Winston Churchill, of certain British scientists to his penthouse in the Shoreham Hotel in Washington. There, the British handed over to Loomis a suitcase containing their knowledge of microwave radar. With the Battle of Britain raging, Loomis' microwave expertise enabled him to grasp immediately the military implications of the technology for air warfare. He promptly persuaded his cousin and mentor, Secretary of War Henry Stimson (who ever doubted the power of WASP family connections?) that this technology must be developed and exploited without delay. With Bush and Roosevelt's immediate approval, Loomis set up the Radiation Laboratory at

MIT in a matter of weeks. Drawing on the connections he had formed at his Tuxedo Park lab, Loomis and his friend Ernest Lawrence were able to convince nearly all they telephoned in the top talent base of U.S. physicists to join the Rad Lab. Because the U.S. government was not accustomed to establishing major labs overnight, Loomis personally funded the start-up until government approvals and procurement caught up.

The Rad Lab used a talent base with a mix of science disciplines and technology skills. The highly collaborative lab was nonhierarchical, with only two levels: project managers and project teams. Each "great group" team was devoted to a particular technology path. Each was organized around a problem-solving approach to a powerful technology challenge. The Rad Lab deployed a management effort that connected the stages of research, development, prototyping, and initial production. The teams worked intense and long hours and did so in high spirits. Loomis and Bush purposely kept the lab out of military uniform and reach. Before long, the Rad Lab had developed microwave radar as well as other advances that led, for example, to the proximity fuse, which enabled a shell to explode when near a target such as a high-speed aircraft. The Rad Lab produced eleven Nobel laureates over five years, formed the organizational model for the development of the atomic bomb at Los Alamos, and laid some of the foundations for modern electronics.

To provide the space for this reservoir of core talent to succeed, Vannevar Bush created the surrounding organizational foundation—first the National Defense Research Council and then the Office of Science Research and Development.[4] Bush brought all defense research efforts under this one loose coordinating tent, which housed the Rad Lab and other research projects, and set up nonbureaucratic, interdisciplinary project teams oriented to the major technology challenges of the day as implementing task forces. He created "connected science," where technology breakthroughs at the fundamental science stage were closely connected to follow-on, applied stages of development, prototyping, and production, operating under what could be called a technological challenge model. Because Bush and Loomis could get direct support from President Roosevelt through Secretary Stimson and presidential aide Harry Hopkins, Bush made his organizational model stick throughout the war, despite relentless pressure from the uniformed services—especially the U.S. Navy—to capture it.

Immediately after the war, Bush systematically dismantled his remarkable connected-science creation. Envisioning a period of world peace, he was convinced that wartime levels of government science investment would be slashed. He probably also was wary of a permanent alliance between the military and science. Bush decided, however, to try to salvage some residual level of federal science investment. He had written for Roosevelt in late 1944 the most influential polemic in the history of American science: "Science: The Endless Frontier."[5] In that masterful essay Bush argued that the U.S. government should fund basic research, which would deliver continual progress in economic well-being and national security. In other words, he proposed ending his wartime model of connected-science research and development organized around major technology challenges in favor of making the federal role one of funding only a single stage of technology advance: basic research.

Bush's approach became known as the "pipeline" model for science investment. The federal government would dump basic science into one end of an innovation pipeline. Somehow, early- and late-stage technology development and prototyping would occur inside the pipeline, and new technology products would magically emerge at the other end. Bush must have realized the deep connection problems inherent in the pipeline model, but he probably reasoned that salvaging federal basic-research investment was the best he could achieve in the coming period of peace.

Bush did argue that this basic research approach should be organized and coordinated under one tent to direct all the nation's research portfolios. To this end he proposed the creation of what became the National Science Foundation (NSF). Bush strongly wanted this entity to be controlled by a scientific elite separate from the nation's political leadership—and certainly separate from its generals and admirals—and he fell into a quarrel with Roosevelt's successor, Harry Truman, on this point. In his characteristically feisty, take-charge way, Truman insisted that the scientific buck would stop on his desk, not on that of some Brahmin scientist. Truman wanted the president to control key NSF appointments; Bush disagreed.

Truman therefore vetoed Bush's NSF legislation, stalling its creation for another five years. Meanwhile, science and science organizing in the U.S. government did not stand still. New agencies proliferated, and the outbreak of the Korean War led to a renewal of specifically defense-science efforts. By the time the NSF was established and funded in 1950, its potential coordinating role had in effect been bypassed. It also became a much smaller agency than Bush had anticipated, and only one among many—Bush's one-tent model had gone by the boards. Instead, the government adopted a highly decentralized model for its science endeavors.[6] Bush's concept of federal funding focused on basic science did prevail, however, as most of the new science agencies adopted the pipeline model.

These twin developments left U.S. science fragmented at the institutional level in two ways: overall science organization was split among numerous science agencies; but federal investment was focused only on one stage of the technological pipeline—exploratory basic research. Bush thus left a legacy of two conflicting models for science organization: the connected, challenge model of World War II; and the basic science-focused, disconnected, multiheaded model that followed. In short, science became very convoluted.

DARPA Rising

DARPA reversed this legacy. President Dwight D. Eisenhower created DARPA in 1957 to be a unifying force for defense R&D. Eisenhower, who also initiated the Solarium exercise in 1953 that led to an early articulation of a coherent U.S. strategy for the cold war, rarely gets credit for being a postwar organizational master—but a master he surely was. Eisenhower beheld the military services' stovepiped, disconnected space programs that had led to America's loss of the space satellite race to Sputnik and demanded change.

Thanks to Eisenhower's initiative, DARPA became a unique entity. In many ways, DARPA directly inherited the connected-science, challenge, and great-group organization models of the Rad Lab and Los Alamos. Unlike these models, which operated primarily on the personal level, DARPA has operated at the institutional level as well. DARPA became a bridge connecting the institutional and personal organizational elements, unlike any other R&D entity.

The DARPA model is perhaps best illustrated by one of its most successful practitioners, J. C. R. Licklider. As a DARPA project manager, Licklider founded and worked with a series of great technology teams, laying the foundations for two of the twentieth century's technology revolutions—personal computing and the Internet.[7] He is that rare example of the technology visionary becoming the vision enabler.

In 1960 Licklider, who was trained in psychology as well as physics and mathematics, wrote about what he called the "man-machine interface" and "human-computer symbiosis": "The hope is that in not too many years, human brains and computing machines will be coupled together very tightly, and that the resulting partnership will think as no human brain has ever thought."[8] He envisioned real-time personal computing (as opposed to the then-dominant mainframe computing model), digital libraries, and the Internet (he called it the "Intergalactic Computer Network"). He also foresaw most of the personal computing functions now taken for granted—graphing, simulations, modeling, and more.

These insights served Licklider well in the new assignment coming his way. President John F. Kennedy and Defense Secretary Robert McNamara were deeply frustrated by the profound command-and-control problems they encountered during the Cuban missile crisis, particularly the inability to obtain and analyze real-time data and interact with on-the-scene military commanders. DARPA called on Licklider, already at the agency, to tackle the problem. Strongly backed by noted early DARPA directors Jack Ruina and Charles Herzfeld, Licklider set in place a remarkable support network of early information technology researchers at universities and firms that, over time, built the sinews of personal computing and the Internet.

At the institutional level, DARPA and Licklider became a collaborative force throughout the 1960s and 1970s among Defense Department research agencies controlled by the uniformed services. They used DARPA investments to leverage their participation to solve common problems using the connected science and technological challenge models. DARPA and Licklider also kept their own research bureaucracy to a bare minimum, using the service R&D agencies to carry out project management and administrative tasks. Institutionally, DARPA became more a research supporter and collaborator and less a rival to the Defense Department research establishment. DARPA also provided an institutional example within the Defense Department for creating a flexible, cross-agency, cross-discipline model among the separate U.S. R&D agencies. At the personal level, meanwhile, Licklider created not only a remarkable base of information technology talent within DARPA, but also, through the vehicle of DARPA contracts, a major collaborative network of great research groups around the country.

Even that is not quite all. Because DARPA was willing to patiently nurture long-term R&D investments in a way that corporations and venture capital firms were not, Licklider's DARPA model came with a native capacity for self-renewal. DARPA internally institutionalized innovation so that successive generations of talent would sustain the information technology revolution over the long term. The great groups Licklider started shared key features of the Rad Lab groups that came before; his Information Processing Techniques group remains the first and greatest success of the DARPA model. But this was not its only success. DARPA also achieved similar accomplishments in other technology areas, supporting remarkable advances in such areas as stealth; high-energy lasers; robotics; and computer hardware, software, and chip fabrication.[9]

Finally, DARPA was eager to catalyze technology advances not only in the defense sector but in the civilian economy as well. Its directors, senior scientists, and managers recognized that an entire economy has to embrace innovation for the defense sector to thrive. The Department of Defense was thus able to take advantage of a broad acceleration of technology development. By seeding the private sector, DARPA reduced the department's development and acquisition costs over a range of military-relevant technologies. But beyond that, the department acquired assets it had never imagined. When Andrew Marshall, the Defense Department's legendary in-house defense theorist and head of its Office of Net Assessment, argued in the late 1980s that U.S. forces were creating a "revolution in military affairs," this defense transformation was built around many of the information technology breakthroughs DARPA initially sponsored. At the same time, these information technology innovations originally sponsored because of their military utility ended up spurring an unprecedented innovation wave that swept into the U.S. economy in the 1990s, creating strong productivity gains and new business models in dozens of industries. These in turn have led to a vast creation of new societal wealth that is still funding ongoing defense transformation. In short, DARPA has created a new Appian Way.

The Innovation Model

What, then, does a successful innovation organization look like "in the raw," so to speak? If the U.S. government ever finds the good sense to apply the DARPA model to the country's energy problem, what would, or should, the skeletal organization of a Manhattan Project, or more accurately a series of such projects, for energy look like?

As DARPA has shown, it would have to work at two levels: the institutional and the personal. And it would be wise to take to heart DARPA's twelve organizing elements:[10]

—*Small and flexible*: DARPA consists of only 100–150 professionals; some observers have referred to DARPA as "100 geniuses connected by a travel agent."

—*Flat organization*: DARPA avoids military hierarchy, essentially operating at only two levels to ensure participation.

—*Autonomy and freedom from bureaucratic impediments*: DARPA operates outside the civil-service hiring process and standard government contracting rules, a situation that gives it unusual access to talent, plus speed and flexibility in organizing R&D efforts.

—*Eclectic, world-class technical staff*: DARPA seeks great talent, drawn from industry, universities, and government laboratories and R&D centers, mixing disciplines as well as theoretical and experimental strengths. This talent has been hybridized through joint corporate-academic collaborations.

—*Teams and networks*: At its very best, DARPA creates and sustains great teams of researchers who are networked to collaborate and share in the team's advances, so that DARPA operates at the personal, face-to-face level of innovation. DARPA is not simply about funding research; its program managers are dynamic playwrights and directors.

—*Hiring continuity and change*: DARPA's technical staff members are hired or assigned for three to five years. Like any strong organization, DARPA mixes experience and change. It retains a base of experienced experts who know their way around the Defense Department, but rotates most of its staff from the outside to ensure fresh thinking and perspectives.

—*Project-based assignments, organized around a challenge model*: DARPA organizes a significant part of its portfolio around specific technology challenges. It works "right-to-left" in the R&D pipeline, foreseeing new innovation-based capabilities and then working back to the fundamental breakthroughs that take them there. Although its projects typically last three to five years, major technological challenges may be addressed over much longer time periods, ensuring patient, long-term investment on a series of focused steps and keeping teams together for ongoing collaboration.

—*Outsourced support personnel*: DARPA uses technical, contracting, and administrative services from other agencies on a temporary basis. This provides DARPA with the flexibility to get into and out of a technology field without the burden of sustaining staff, while building cooperative alliances with the line agencies with which it works.

—*Outstanding program managers*: In DARPA's words, "the best DARPA program managers have always been freewheeling zealots in pursuit of their goals." The DARPA director's most important job historically has been to recruit highly talented program managers and then empower their creativity to put together great teams around great advances.

—*Acceptance of failure*: At its best, DARPA pursues a high-risk model for breakthrough opportunities and is very tolerant of failure if the payoff from potential success is great enough.

—*Orientation to revolutionary breakthroughs in a connected approach*: DARPA historically has focused not on incremental but on radical innovation. It emphasizes high-risk investment, moves from fundamental technological advances to prototyping, and then hands off the production stage to the armed services or the commercial sector. From an institutional innovation perspective, DARPA is a connected model, crossing the barriers between innovation stages.

—*Mix of connected collaborators*: DARPA typically builds strong teams and networks of collaborators, bringing in a range of technical expertise and applicable disciplines and involving university researchers and technology firms that are usually not significant defense contractors or Beltway consultants (neither of which focuses on radical innovation). The aim of DARPA's "hybrid" approach, unique among American R&D agencies, is to ensure strong collaborative "mindshare" on the challenge and the capability to connect fundamentals with applications.

A DARPA Energy Franchise

The challenge now is to take these twelve essentials of innovation organization and create a new agency for energy technology innovation—perhaps associated with a reinvigorated Department of Energy—that can do for energy innovation what DARPA has done for military innovation. The evolution of alternative energy technology has been sporadic, and technology transition has been glacial; a connected DARPA model is a way to attack both problems. The National Academy's noteworthy 2006 report, *Rising above the Gathering Storm*, has called for exactly this. They call it—surprise!—ARPA-E: Advanced Research Projects Agency–Energy. Authorization to establish ARPA-E is now rattling around Congress in various bills.

It is important to remember, above all, the key to the DARPA model's success: DARPA has served a keystone function, bringing talent and appropriate infrastructure together—and then getting out of the way.[11] By avoiding a heavy institutional footprint and all forms of "landlord" status (mere rent collecting from past technological exploits), DARPA has been able to renew itself continuously without getting weighed down by legacy projects or staff (although some observers are arguing that DARPA itself is now abandoning its own model). It is clear that any legislation designed to set up ARPA-E must mandate DARPA-like characteristics from the outset. Legislation that is too generally drawn and given over to bureaucrats to flesh out will almost certainly lead to the wholesale violation of the twelve characteristics listed here, and thence to the headlong failure of the entire enterprise. For example, legislation has to stipulate a flat entity, with only two levels to ensure productive collaboration. Project managers must be left in control of their research and development agendas and budgets. There must be absolutely no budget-office layer between the director and his project managers. It is also crucial that any

ARPA-E director have direct and prompt access to departmental leadership—ARPA-E must not become a subordinate office to a larger R&D entity at the departmental level.

Obviously, however, significant differences exist between the environment in which DARPA has operated and those in which a DARPA energy clone would operate. DARPA launched its breakthrough information technologies largely into niche sectors that faced limited initial competitive pressures and could be supported by the new model DARPA itself helped to encourage, of start-ups, entrepreneurs, venture capital, and angel capital. Some new disruptive energy technologies could be launched into this niche realm, while others face profound competitive pressures from an entrenched energy sector that will resist them. There is also no single silver energy-technology bullet. Energy is a highly complex system so the single technology focus of the Manhattan Project will not work; a range of new technology introductions is required to meet needs in transport, electricity, and efficiency. Another difference is that DARPA has an initial "customer" for many of its products. The Defense Department procurement base is, after all, enormous. ARPA-E's eventual products could have a significant government-based customer, if, for example, Congress ordered all new federal construction to integrate revolutionary solar nanotechnology membranes for electrical power generation or directed military transport to slash its fuel consumption with hybrids featuring powerful new nanotech batteries. But ARPA-E would not have a government customer base nearly as large as DARPA's. Nevertheless, even in some niche areas it could have a nongovernment customer base that is orders of magnitude larger than the Defense Department. Because of the complexity of the energy sector, a new energy R&D entity is only part of the puzzle, but it is a critical initial step—new technologies are the prerequisite to other governmental interventions.

Given these realities, it would be wise to begin construction of ARPA-E by seconding seasoned veterans of DARPA to it. An agency is its culture, not just its enabling statute or organizational chart. Only those who have worked within the DARPA culture understand it well enough to lead and mentor the first generation of ARPA-E senior staff. (A major error was made when the Department of Homeland Security's Science and Technology Directorate, which was to follow the DARPA model, failed to empower its ex-DARPA veterans.)

What are the institutional barriers to a DARPA clone at the Department of Energy? The first barrier is fear. The existing national energy labs, no longer needing to work flat out on building new generations of nuclear weapons and searching for new missions, dread an in-house competitor. To survive at the Energy Department, ARPA-E instead will have to be perceived as a collaborator, potentially seeding new technologies with the national energy labs, just as DARPA seeded the established service R&D organizations. It cannot become just another national energy lab or support its own infrastructure; it must be light and flexible, operating as a connector for the established labs and building its own strong teams of personal-level tech enablers. It cannot simply fund existing labs, either. It will have to break some lab china by providing, like DARPA, strong funding for competing corporate-academic research groups. An energy transformation demands new entrants, not just the existing cast of characters. The best lab talent understands that the labs need more competitive pressure because too little technology is transitioning from them into the commercial sector. The ARPA-E name already carries heavy baggage within the Department of Energy—it can be changed. The important thing is not choosing the name, but rather understanding how and why the DARPA model has worked so well and adopting the right form of its twelve essentials for success. Given the vast size of the current energy infrastructure and capital plant, it will take time for any breakthrough innovations to be widely adopted. So we need to begin as soon as possible.

Finally, there is no inherent reason why other DARPA clones—bioscience under the heavily stovepiped National Institutes of Health, for example—could not also be created. That would depend, of course, on leadership in both the executive and legislative branches. If the current administration and congressional leadership do not appreciate the importance of bold investment in the future of American science and technology—and clearly there is a problem here, with the administration's first, extremely modest competitiveness initiative still languishing in Congress after six years in office —perhaps another era of political leadership will. It is not simply a matter of R&D investment levels; innovation organization is also important. We must apply the organization lessons we have already learned.

How important is innovation organization to America's national power and economic health? Let me end as I began, by considering ancient Rome. Roman children played with a toy called an aeolipile, made up of a metal ball suspended by pins on each side so that it could spin freely; the water-filled ball had directional nozzles on the top and bottom. When the water in the ball was heated, steam would jet out and spin the ball. The aeolipile was, in short, a rudimentary steam engine.

Imagine if some innovative Roman had envisioned this child's toy enlarged and hooked to a set of wheels moving under its own power on the Appian Way. As it happened, there was no such Roman. Rome lacked the scientific institutions to capitalize on this latent technology, precisely the function for which DARPA has been organized. Think of the loss that results when a society fails to dedicate itself to innovation, even when the organizational tools are at hand. What a waste, and how embarrassing to posterity.

7

Fueled Again? In Search of Energy Security

Gal Luft and Anne Korin

On February 17, 2006, a rebel group called the Movement for the Emancipation of the Niger Delta (MEND) declared "total war" against oil companies operating in Nigeria's main oil-producing region. Nigeria is Africa's leading oil exporter and ranks fifth as an oil supplier to the United States. For oil companies, it is one of the most inhospitable domains on the planet in which to do business. In recent years the country, half of which is controlled by strict Islamic law, has become a cauldron of turmoil where sectarian violence, radicalism, and corruption are rampant and on the rise.

That winter week, MEND launched a campaign of pipeline sabotage and kidnapping of oil workers that led to a 20 percent decline in Nigeria's oil production. Five days later, Iraq, the world's second largest reserve of conventional crude, nearly went offline when the Shi'a Askaria shrine in Samarra was bombed, pushing the country into a bloody civil war. Since Saddam Hussein's invasion of Kuwait in August 1990, Iraq has been producing far less oil than its potential capacity. Years of sanctions and neglect had brought production to under three million barrels a day, and the Iraq war has since brought the country to a new oil production low. A sabotage campaign against the country's oil installations has reduced Iraqi production to a disappointing average of two million barrels a day. But the Samarra attack could have pushed the country over the edge, stopping crude exports altogether. This was the moment al-Qaeda was waiting for.

Since September 11, 2001, terrorist groups have identified oil terrorism as a way to break the economic backbone of the West. Until 2002 the oil market had sufficient elasticity to deal with occasional supply disruptions. Such disruptions could be offset by the spare production capacity owned by some members of OPEC (Organization of Petroleum Exporting Countries), chiefly Saudi Arabia. This spare capacity has been the oil market's main source of liquidity. But burgeoning demand in developing Asia coupled with voracious appetites of traditional consumers in the industrialized world have together eroded this liquidity mechanism from seven million barrels a day in 2002, which constituted 10 percent of the market, to about two million barrels today, less than 2.5 percent. As a result, the oil market today resembles a car without shock absorbers: the tiniest bump can send a passenger to the ceiling.

Without liquidity, the only mechanism left to bring the market to equilibrium is rapid and uncontrolled price increases. This reality plays into the hands of jihadists who seek to hurt the Western economy by going after what they call "the provision line and the feeding to the artery of the life of the crusader's nation." In an October 2004 videotape, Osama bin Laden explained: "We bled Russia for ten years until it went bankrupt and was forced to withdraw [from Afghanistan] in defeat. . . . We are continuing in the same policy to make America bleed profusely to the point of bankruptcy." And that is why, throughout the world, jihadi terrorists have been attacking oil facilities almost on a daily basis, with significant impact on the oil market.

On a normal day these attacks impose a "fear premium" on the oil market of around $10–$15 a barrel. For the United States, an importer of twelve million barrels a day, this fear premium alone costs roughly $50 billion a year. But in February 2006, the combination of unrest in Nigeria and Iraq and fear over a looming crisis with Iran presented al-Qaeda with a unique opportunity to deliver a crippling blow to the global economy by preventing a significant amount of oil supply from reaching the market. That could be done most effectively by an attack on a strategic oil installation in Saudi Arabia. So on February 24, 2006, two trucks, driven by suicide bombers and each laden with one ton of explosives, blew up at the outer perimeter of Saudi Arabia's Abqaiq—the world's largest oil-processing facility, through which more than half of Saudi oil passes each and every day.

Luckily, the terrorists failed to cause significant damage to the plant. But had they succeeded in turning the complex into an inferno, they would have denied the world roughly half of Saudi Arabia's oil and its remaining spare capacity. That would amount to more oil than all the OPEC members took off the market during the 1973–74 Arab oil embargo. Had such a calamity happened in conjunction with the shutdowns in Nigeria and Iraq, oil prices would have soared to $150–$200 a barrel. If it had happened in the midst of a hurricane season or an extra-cold winter, the outcome would have been even more catastrophic for the United States. Studies and simulations show that a loss of as little as three million barrels a day can cause gasoline prices to double, resulting in a loss of more than one million jobs in the United States alone and a significant spike in the current account deficit. If not for three factors—the terrorists' incompetence, responsible behavior by Iraq's Shi'a clerics who calmed things down, and the Nigerian military—February 2006 could have ended with a far larger loss.

For the U.S. economy and the world economy at large, the danger of simultaneous multiple failures in the global oil industry could be more economically damaging than an outbreak of a pandemic or a dirty bomb set off in New York City. The supply disruptions of the 1970s cost the U.S. economy between $2.3 trillion and $2.5 trillion.[1] According to the National Defense Council Foundation, a disruption of similar proportions today could carry a price tag as high as $8 trillion—a figure equal to more than 60 percent of U.S. annual gross domestic product, or nearly $27,000 for every man, woman, and child living in America.[2] This is more money than the United States has spent in all of its wars combined since 1776. The fact that ten of the top fourteen oil-exporting countries are politically unstable, that the United States may be facing a long period of increased hurricane activity in the Gulf of Mexico, and that, following the Abqaiq attack, al-Qaeda promised that "we shall not cease our attacks until our territories are liberated," implies that it is only a matter of time before the United States finds itself in the midst of a severe oil shock.[3] Here is an eminently predictable catastrophe if ever there was one.

The Energy Weapon Is Back

Transportation underlies the modern U.S. economy. With 97 percent of U.S. transportation energy based on petroleum, oil is the lifeblood of America's economy. Without oil, goods and raw materials cannot reach their destinations, service providers cannot arrive at their clients, and children cannot go to school. America is poor in oil relative to its need. It consumes one of every four gallons in the world but has barely 3 percent of the world's proven reserves. The United States now imports 60 percent of its oil, more than twice as much as it imported before the 1973–74 Arab oil embargo. While America grows increasingly dependent on this resource, its supply to households and industries is ever more threatened, not only by nonstate actors like MEND, al-Qaeda, and the Iraqi insurgents, but also by the swaggering of oil-producing nations.

Conventional wisdom holds that the oil weapon used against the United States and its allies in the 1970s is obsolete. While it is true that the OPEC states that wielded the oil weapon subsequently suffered the most from it, the assumption that this weapon will not be used again is dangerous considering that in the past five years alone, no fewer than six energy exporters unsheathed the oil saber when tension with the United States deepened. In October 2002, member countries of the Organization of the Islamic Conference considered an oil embargo as a way to stop the United States from attacking Iraq. Mahathir Mohamad, then Malaysia's prime minister, said: "Oil is the only thing Muslim nations have which is needed by the rest of the world. . . . [By cutting back supply] it can be used as a weapon to protect the interest of Muslims."[4] Earlier, in April 2002, Saddam Hussein declared an oil embargo for thirty days in response to Israeli military operations in the West Bank. Libya immediately announced that it would follow suit if other Muslim oil-producers imposed an oil embargo. Iran's supreme leader Ayatollah Ali Khamenei reminded his OPEC colleagues that if the West did not receive oil, "their factories would grind to a halt. This will shake the world!"[5] A day later, similar sounds came from Saudi Arabia. More recently, Venezuela's president, Hugo Chávez, has twice threatened to cut off oil shipments to the United States, and some senior Iranian officials have threatened to block the flow of oil from the Persian Gulf if the United Nations imposes sanctions over Tehran's nuclear-weapons program. In one case, Russia cut the supply of gas to Ukraine as punishment for its movement toward democracy.

This trend is alarming because it shows a growing inclination on the part of energy producers to use a negotiating method that for the past three decades has been taboo. More unsettling is the fact that in the future the industrialized world will be much more beholden to oil and gas exporters, particularly to OPEC. While non-OPEC countries pump at full speed, OPEC producers stick to a quota. As a result, the former are depleting their oil reserves proportionately faster than OPEC. ExxonMobil Corporation has estimated that non-OPEC production—this includes Russia and West Africa (excluding Nigeria, which belongs to OPEC)—will peak within a decade.[6] At that point, there will be little easily recoverable oil left outside of the Middle East or, as the International Energy Agency put it in November 2005, "We are ending up with 95 percent of the world relying for its economic well being on decisions made by five or six countries in the Middle East."[7]

"Warping" Foreign Policy

Deeply embroiled in a struggle against radical Islam, nuclear proliferation, and totalitarianism, the United States faces a crude reality: While its relations with the Muslim world are at an all-time low, more than 70 percent of the world's proven oil reserves and over a third of production are concentrated in Muslim countries. The very same Shi'a and Sunni theocratic and dictatorial regimes that most strongly resist America's efforts to bring democracy to the Middle East are the ones that, because of the market's tightness, currently drive the world oil economy. While the U.S. economy bleeds, oil-producing countries like Saudi Arabia and Iran—sympathetic to, if not directly supportive of, radical Islam—are on the receiving end of staggering windfalls. In 2005 the United States spent more than $251 billion on foreign crude oil and refined petroleum products. In 2007, with oil hovering between $60 and $70 a barrel, the figure could surpass $300 billion. Not only are U.S. oil imports the cause of about a third of the U.S. trade deficit, but they are also an indirect contributor to the spread of radical Islam and antidemocracy forces. An undetermined portion of the petrodollars sent to the Middle East finds its way—through official and unofficial government handouts, charities, and well-connected businesses—to the jihadists committed to America's destruction. On July 13, 2005, Undersecretary of the Treasury Stuart Levey told the Senate Committee on Banking, Housing and Urban Affairs that "wealthy Saudi financiers and charities have funded terrorist organizations and causes that support terrorism and the ideology that fuels the terrorists' agenda. Even today, we believe that Saudi donors may still be a significant source of terrorist financing, including for the insurgency in Iraq."[8]

The flow of petrodollars from consuming economies to the coffers of producers that, in the words of President George W. Bush, "don't particularly like us," not only casts a large shadow over America's prospects of winning the war on terrorism but also limits U.S. diplomatic maneuverability on central issues like human rights and nuclear proliferation. Perhaps the most powerful statement of the impact on America's ability to accomplish its foreign policy goals came from Secretary of State Condoleezza Rice, who in April 2006 told the Senate Foreign Relations Committee:

> We do have to do something about the energy problem. I can tell you that nothing has really taken me aback more, as Secretary of State, than the way that the politics of energy is . . . "warping" diplomacy around the world. It has given extraordinary power to some states that are using

> that power in not very good ways for the international system, states that would otherwise have very little power.[9]

One of these states is Iran. With 10 percent of the world's oil reserves and the world's second largest natural gas reserve, Iran's President Mahmoud Ahmadinejad seems unfazed by the prospects of international sanctions against his country as a result of its efforts to develop nuclear weapons. With high oil prices, leaders of human-rights-violating countries like Azerbaijan, Chad, Sudan, Turkmenistan, and Uzbekistan, too, can persecute their people with impunity. The control over a large part of the world's oil and gas market allows Russia's president Vladimir Putin to bully his European neighbors, to play "hard to get" on Iran, and to undermine democracy in former Soviet republics like Georgia and Ukraine.

Oil also lubricates the so-called Bolivarian revolution led by Venezuela's Chávez, who is using his country's oil wealth to buy political influence in the Western Hemisphere and to consolidate an anti-U.S. bloc in the region. In 2005, he signed agreements to finance cheap oil to thirteen Caribbean countries, bought up more than $1 billion of Argentina's debt, and worked to distance Mexico from the United States. At the same time Chávez is leading a nationalization campaign against multinational energy companies operating in South America, which will surely discourage energy majors from making the investments necessary to develop the region's economies.

U.S. diplomacy is further complicated by the indefatigable thirst for energy of emerging countries like China and India, which are becoming increasingly dependent on the very same countries the United States is trying to rein in. The growing appetite of developing Asian powers not only plays into the hands of the aforementioned rogue producing nations, but also feeds what could become a global competition for control of energy resources.

Foreign Policy Begins in Our Garage

The unique strategic importance of oil to the modern economy—beyond that of any other commodity today—stems from the fact that the global economy's very enabler, the transportation sector, is utterly dependent on it, with 220 million cars and trucks in the United States alone. Today's vehicles have an average life span of sixteen years and, for the most part, can run only on petroleum. Therefore, even if every new vehicle produced runs on some alternative fuel, uninterrupted supplies of conventional fuels will still be needed for the next fifteen to twenty years.

The petroleum industry will doubtless do its part: With high oil prices expected for the foreseeable future, Americans are likely to see expanded domestic production using enhanced recovery technologies; the government relaxing some restrictions on domestic drilling; and, increasingly, nonconventional sources of petroleum such as tar sands, extra-heavy oil, and oil shale coming online. An estimated 180 billion barrels of oil can potentially be generated from tar sands in Canada, and technology is being developed to tap an additional 800 billion barrels of oil from shale in Colorado, Utah, and Wyoming—more than triple the proven oil reserves of Saudi Arabia. America's vast coal reserves can also be tapped to produce synthetic petroleum. A process called Fischer-Tropsch, which was used extensively by Nazi Germany and by South Africa, allows the conversion of coal to clean diesel. The process is economically viable with oil selling at $45 per barrel and above; the U.S. Department of Energy estimates that by 2030 a tenth of current U.S. oil production will come from coal.[10] These solutions will require significant investment in the United States and abroad. The International Energy Agency estimates that it will take $16 trillion in spending, much of it by national and privately owned oil companies, over the next twenty-five years on new energy infrastructure just to keep up with growing demand and to insulate the world from shocks.[11]

On the demand side of the equation, industrialized nations have demonstrated a remarkable ability to conserve and improve efficiency once prices spike. In response to OPEC's oil embargo, U.S. oil consumption fell 15 percent between 1979 and 1985, and oil imports fell by 42 percent. Because 60 percent of the projected increase in oil use in the next twenty years will be in the transportation sector, the biggest efficiency gains can be accomplished there. Roughly 40 percent of the world's supply goes to power cars and trucks. Public policy initiatives—such as gasoline taxes; fuel efficiency standards for cars and trucks; and, in response to crisis, the introduction of mild austerity measures—could dampen demand and push prices down. After fuel economy standards were introduced in the United States in 1978, the fuel efficiency of new cars and trucks rose quickly, though it has leveled off in recent years. The introduction of hybrid technology, which combines an internal combustion engine with an electric motor, allows auto manufacturers to increase efficiency without compromising safety or performance. Because of their high efficiency, hybrid electric vehicles can attain between 20 percent to over twice the mileage of conventional gasoline engines. In the more distant future the introduction of extra-strong lightweight vehicle materials could improve efficiency even further.[12]

But neither efforts to expand petroleum supply nor those to crimp petroleum demand will be enough to reduce America's strategic vulnerability anytime soon. When the British Navy made the shift from coal to oil, then Lord of the Admiralty Winston Churchill famously remarked, "safety and certainty in oil lies in variety and variety alone." To diminish the strategic importance of oil to the international system it is now critical to expand the Churchillian doctrine beyond geographical variety to a variety of fuels.

The United States and other major oil-consuming countries are well endowed with a variety of energy resources, including coal (the United States has a quarter of the world's total reserves); agricultural, municipal, and industrial waste; dedicated energy crops; nuclear power; and solar and wind power. All of these energy sources can play a role in the transportation system as part of what might be called a "fuel choice" strategy.

The key to fuel choice is the deployment of multifuel vehicle technologies that are readily available and compatible with the nation's current energy infrastructure. One key technology is the flex-fuel vehicle. This feature, which adds only $150 to the cost of a new car, enables the use of any combination of gasoline and alcohols such as ethanol and methanol. About six million such cars are already on America's roads. In Brazil, where ethanol is widely used, the share of new car sales that have fuel flexibility has risen from 4 percent to 67 percent in just three years.

Where will the fuel come from? Throughout the world alternative fuels today total a mere 2 percent of the transportation fuel market. But rising oil prices have brought a spike in demand and production of gasoline replacements. Ethanol production has more than doubled since 2000; production of biodiesel fuel has expanded nearly threefold. In many countries, motor fuel is already blended with ethanol. In Brazil, for example, ethanol accounts today for 20 percent of the country's transportation fuel market.[13] According to the Worldwatch Institute, the world could theoretically harvest enough biomass to satisfy the total anticipated global demand for transportation fuels by 2050.[14]

In the United States today ethanol is made primarily from corn. Hopes of drastically ramping up domestic production are predicated on the commercialization of advanced technologies to convert cellulosic material like switch grass, wood chips, and rice straw to ethanol using genetically modified biocatalysts. In his 2006 State of the Union address, President Bush set a goal for such technologies to mature in under six years. Until this happens, the United States should use sugar cane as well as corn for ethanol production. Sugar yields five times more energy than corn and costs half the price to turn into ethanol. Therefore, unlike corn, it does not require a government subsidy (in today's climate of high prices, with production costs of corn ethanol well under $1.50 a gallon and selling costs about $2.30, it is questionable whether corn ethanol requires its current subsidies).

Unfortunately, the United States does not have an ideal climate for growing sugar cane—sugar needs a long, frost-free growing season—and is not able to ramp up sugar production to the level needed to even come close to satisfying its energy needs. This is why Latin American and Caribbean countries like Brazil, Costa Rica, the Dominican Republic, El Salvador, Guatemala, Honduras, and Jamaica—all low-cost sugar cane producers—could become keys to U.S. energy security. Brazil, the Saudi Arabia of sugar, already exports half a billion gallons of ethanol a year and could provide the United States with cheap ethanol. "We don't want to sell liters of ethanol," Brazil's agriculture minister Roberto Rodrigues said in 2004. "We want to sell rivers."[15]

Expanding U.S. fuel choice to include biofuels imported from our neighbors in the Western Hemisphere has significant geopolitical benefits at a time when U.S. standing in the region is challenged. Sugar is now grown in one hundred countries, many of which are poor. Encouraging these countries to increase their output and become fuel suppliers could have far-reaching implications for their economic development. By creating economic interdependence with sugar-producing countries in Africa and the Western Hemisphere, the United States can strengthen its position in the developing world and provide significant help in reducing poverty. In many countries where coca is grown and used for the production of narcotics, sugar could replace coca and thus help address the scourge of the illicit drug trade.[16] Yet despite the economic and geopolitical benefits of sugar ethanol in the United States, corn and sugar growers as well as major ethanol refiners oppose imports of sugar ethanol. The growers' champions in Congress have imposed a stiff tariff of 54 cents a gallon on imported ethanol to protect local industry. The result is that, while fuel imported from Saudi Arabia or Venezuela is not taxed, fuel coming from Brazil is. This is absurd.

A game-changing alcohol that could be used in flexible fuel vehicles is methanol, also known as wood alcohol. While ethanol can be made only from agricultural products like corn, sugar cane, and, assuming technological success, cellulosic biomass, methanol can be made from all of them, plus an array of other carbon-rich energy sources with which the United States is well endowed. Today, about 90 percent of the worldwide methanol supply is produced from methane, the main component of natural gas. Technologies to produce methanol from coal are at hand, and a commercial-scale plant in the United States now produces it for about 50 cents a gallon (methanol has about half the energy of gasoline, so this equates to about $1 a gasoline-equivalent gallon). In China eight provinces have recently made a strategic decision to use methanol as a fuel, and eighty coal-to-methanol plants are in the making. When it comes to biomass, methanol enjoys a significant advantage over ethanol: a ton of biomass will produce 50 percent more energy if converted to methanol than to ethanol. Chemistry Nobel laureate George Olah has also proposed recycling carbon dioxide emissions from industrial exhausts by combining them with nuclear or renewable hydrogen to produce methanol.[17]

No less promising is the use of electricity as a transportation fuel. In most of the industrial world petroleum is no longer used to generate power. Since the 1970s oil-powered generators have been replaced by nuclear reactors, coal-fired power plants, natural gas turbines, solar panels, and wind turbines. Only about 2 percent of U.S. electricity is now generated from oil. Using electricity as a transportation fuel enables the full spectrum of electricity sources to displace petroleum. Plug-in hybrid electric vehicles (PHEVs) are multifuel vehicles that can utilize grid electricity in addition to liquid fuel. PHEVs can be plugged into an electrical outlet and provide the stored energy for much of a typical day's drive. Like the first-generation hybrids currently on the road, plug-ins have a liquid fuel tank and internal combustion engine, so they have the same driving range as a standard car. A person who drives less than the car's electric range in a day could do so exclusively by recharging the battery and seldom have to dip into the fuel tank. Since half the cars on the road in the United States are driven twenty miles a day or less, a plug-in with a twenty-mile-range battery would reduce gasoline consumption significantly. When the charge is used up, the PHEV automatically switches over to running on the engine powered by the liquid in its fuel tank. PHEVs can reach fuel economy levels of 100 miles per gallon of gasoline. If a PHEV is also a flexible-fuel vehicle powered by 85 percent alcohol and 15 percent gasoline, fuel economy could reach over *500 miles per gallon* of gasoline. Ideally, plug-in hybrids would be charged at night in home or apartment garages, when electric utilities have significant reserve capacity. The Electric Power Research Institute estimates that up to *30 percent* of the U.S. vehicle market could shift to plug-in hybrids without needing to install additional baseload electricity-generating capacity.

Thinking out of the Barrel

By shifting to nonpetroleum, next-generation transportation fuels like alcohol, nonpetroleum diesel, and electricity, Americans can reduce the content of gasoline in their tanks and hence reduce their vulnerability to supply disruptions. Today, the United States imports twelve million barrels of oil a day, and that figure is projected to rise to twenty million by 2025. If all cars on the road by 2025 are either diesels burning some nonpetroleum fuel or flexible and plug-in hybrid vehicles, U.S. oil consumption would drop by as much as twelve million barrels a day. Oil would face competition at the pump with other energy sources, which should serve to dampen its strategic value, enabling America to regain control over its foreign policy and reduce its vulnerability to an energy catastrophe.

A nationwide deployment of flex-fuel cars, plug-in hybrids, and alternative fuels could take place within two decades. But such a transformation will not occur by itself. In a perfect world government would not need to intervene in the energy market, but in a time of war, the United States is taking an unacceptable risk by leaving the problem to be solved by the invisible hand. This is especially true since the energy market is anything but free. It is manipulated by a cartel, heavily rigged in favor of the status quo, and, as the case of Brazilian ethanol shows, riddled with protectionism. In the absence of appropriate public policy, hundreds of millions of petroleum-burning cars ill-suited to address the changing geopolitics and geology of oil will roll onto our roads in coming decades, with profound implications for the future. On pure national security grounds, government must facilitate energy security by requiring that vehicles sold in the United States be able to run on other fuels in addition to oil-based fuel. A fuel-choice standard would level the playing field and promote free competition among diverse energy suppliers.

The shift from an oil-based economy to a fuel-choice economy is a big idea. But the American people have never shied away from big ideas. Space exploration, disease eradication, and the proliferation of freedom were all big ideas that have benefited billions of people around the world. They all required dedicated and enthusiastic leadership, public support, close international cooperation, and, more than anything, perseverance. An aggressive, inventive energy policy can gradually diminish the role of oil in world politics and reduce predictable friction between consumers and producers and among consumers themselves. Such a vision is both practical and economical—far cheaper than maintaining the current energy system. The only question is whether our leaders will lead or will instead be dragged to act by the most painful oil shock in American history.

8

Emerging Infectious Diseases: Are We Prepared?

Scott Barrett

News that a person has become infected with HIV is a personal tragedy but of no consequence to the world at large. News of the *first* person to be infected with HIV—now that, had it been revealed years ago at the start of the pandemic, would have been of monumental importance.

HIV/AIDS was discovered in 1981, in San Francisco, long after the disease had already spread around the world, having probably emerged in Africa fifty years before that. Had the first person infected—the "index case," epidemiologists call him—been identified and prevented from infecting other people, tens of millions of lives would have been saved.

Today, the search is on for the sources of another emerging infectious disease—a pandemic influenza virus. Should the H5N1 bird flu strain mutate to allow human-to-human transmission, this new disease could kill as many people as HIV/AIDS, or more, and in a much shorter period of time. That it has not turned into a mass global killer yet does not mean that it still won't. Many casual observers are under the impression that the absence of a major outbreak in the winter of 2005–06, after a great deal of media attention paid to the prospect, means that the world can now rest easy, that the danger has passed. This is not so.

The 2002 outbreak of severe acute respiratory syndrome (SARS) showed how easily a new disease can spread in today's globalized world. A single infected person, staying at a hotel in Hong Kong, transmitted the disease to at least sixteen other guests and visitors all linked to the same hotel floor, and these persons in turn carried the disease on their travels to Canada, Singapore, and Vietnam. Subsequent waves of transmission spread the disease to thirty countries. Only 916 people died from SARS, but that was due as much to the self-limiting nature of the disease as to the measures taken to contain it.

The pandemic influenza outbreak of 1918–19 spread rapidly, in two waves, helped by the troop movements of World War I. Estimates of the number of people killed by this pandemic vary. The figure of 20 million deaths worldwide is often mentioned, but estimates range as high as 100 million deaths. A new pandemic strain could kill as many people—or more. Modern medicine will help cut fatalities, but the case fatality rate of the H5N1 virus in humans is very high, and the world's population is much greater today, and much more integrated, than it was in 1918.

Society must also contemplate the risk of deliberate release of a toxic biological agent. Terrorists could easily get hold of an agent like anthrax, and they may have already acquired samples of smallpox. Given time, they may be able to develop in the laboratory new, designer pathogens (perhaps crossing the virulence of Ebola with the infectiousness of measles). Polio has already been synthesized in the lab.

All of these emerging infectious diseases—the ones that we can anticipate and the ones that surprise us, the ones that arise by "accidental" mutation and the ones that develop by willful intent, the ones that erupt dramatically and the ones that smolder for years before being detected—all of these pose a dire threat to global health.

Is the world prepared? The United States and other governments have adopted policies and made investments to address these threats, but these steps have been mainly unilateral and defensive when they need also to be global and offensive. A fundamental change in perspective is required to address the threat of emerging infectious diseases. In particular, action is needed in five areas: prevention, preparedness, surveillance, reporting, and response.

Prevention

The human form of bovine spongiform encephalopathy (BSE), or new variant Creutzfeldt-Jakob disease, arose in the United Kingdom because of the practice of rendering cattle offal, including brain and spinal cord tissue, to feed other cattle. Were it not for this rendering process, the original prion mutation—that is, a change in the structure of infectious particles of protein—would not have spread so widely.

Could this risk have been foreseen? Probably not. But diseases that develop from mutations of already-recognized agents can be foreseen—and prevented. The antimalarial drug chloroquine, for example, has lost its effectiveness. Overuse of this drug allowed evolution to select mutations that resist chloroquine, and these new mutations have now spread around the world. Unless decisive action is taken, resistance to the new, artemisinin-based antimalarials will also develop.

To prevent this, global minimum standards should be set. Monotherapy, or single-drug versions, of the new antimalarials should be banned, since they are especially prone to resistance. Multidrug or combination therapies, by contrast, should be subsidized. Currently, neither action is being taken. The World Health Organization has threatened to "name and shame" companies that manufacture and distribute the monotherapies, but that is a weak response. And donor countries have failed to subsidize the new combination therapies. They continue to look at development as requiring investments in particular states rather than as a broader challenge, sometimes with ecological foundations. Chloroquine resistance developed independently in Southeast Asia and South America and spread to Africa, where the *falciparum* form of malaria kills between one million and two million children each year, every year. The nation-centric view of development failed to prevent this disaster.

Actions can also be taken to reduce the risk of an H5N1 mutation that would allow human-to-human transmission. A new mutation could arise if wild migratory birds infected domesticated fowl, these animals then passed a mutation of the disease to humans, and these infected humans in turn transmitted the disease to other humans around the world. Standards that might prevent or at least make less likely this kind of chain event do not exist at the international level. (Indeed, even the European Union has taken a fragmented approach to this current challenge.) The Dutch ordered their commercial poultry flocks indoors to prevent them from being infected by wild, migratory fowl. Nigeria's government, by contrast, could not even identify where the country's largest poultry farms were located.

The essential point is that Nigeria's failure is not only Nigeria's problem. It is *every country's* problem. The United States is just as vulnerable to a pandemic influenza strain that emerges in the outskirts of Lagos as in downtown Chicago.

Note the difference between an emerging infectious disease and a well-established one. By means of mass vaccination, the United States has virtually eliminated measles. It is as if the United States has erected a wall that separates its people from the vulnerable masses in poor countries. Should an infected person enter the United States, almost no Americans will become infected.

Even the people who are not vaccinated will be protected by the herd immunity available in the population. In Africa, by contrast, half a million or so children die every year from this easily preventable disease.

Establishing standards is essential, but so is enforcement. In June 2005 reports surfaced that farmers in China had used an antiviral drug, amantadine, to suppress major bird flu outbreaks, in violation of international livestock guidelines. The consequence is that the H5N1 virus has now become resistant to this drug—and so the countries relying on it (mainly the developing countries) must now turn to more expensive antivirals for treating humans.

To sum up, the challenge of preventing emerging infectious diseases requires collectively agreed, minimum global standards, coupled with assistance with capacity and enforcement.

Preparedness

Prevention is not always possible, and, for the reasons just mentioned, it may be inadequate in any event. So the world must also be prepared to deal with new outbreaks. Preparedness is in every state's self-interest, but it also yields global benefits. This is because preparedness can help limit spread.

Today, countries are stockpiling antiviral drugs and investing in the development of vaccines that, it is hoped, will be effective against a mutation of the H5N1 virus. These measures are to be welcomed, but not every country can afford them—and the countries that fail to invest in preparedness expose the rest of the world to risk. It may not be possible to prevent spread, but even slowing down transmission will be helpful, for it will buy the time needed to develop better tools with which to fight a new influenza strain (the tools available today only guess at the nature of the strain likely to emerge).

Suppose that a new pandemic strain emerges in a developing country that lacks the drugs and vaccines to help slow its spread. Will the countries with stockpiles use them to prevent spread at source, or will they use them defensively to protect their own populations? Stocks are limited and must be rationed, so it is not possible today for countries to do both. Choices will have to be made. If the stocks are used at the source of the outbreak, they will have a greater chance of being effective in slowing global spread. But to deploy them in this fashion would expose the country that donates the drugs and vaccines to a sizable risk.

A global stockpile is therefore needed, and there is one (donated by the manufacturer of the antiviral drug oseltamivir). But the stockpile has only enough to treat three million people. By contrast, the United Kingdom, an island nation with a population of sixty million people, has a stockpile of almost fifteen million doses. What happens if an epidemic of a new bird flu strain emerges in Mumbai, with a population of nearly twenty million people?

Investing in vaccine production capacity is also needed. Current capacity is very limited and located in just a few countries. Should there be an outbreak, where will scarce vaccine stocks be deployed? In the countries where production capacity is based, or where deployment would deliver the greatest global benefit? The world's governments currently lack a global framework for making these crucial decisions.

To summarize: Global preparedness requires a global investment in the tools that can prevent spread at the source of an outbreak, wherever in the world that may be.

Surveillance

Surveillance is needed to identify outbreaks of new diseases. Only when the Centers for Disease Control and Prevention in the United States noticed an unusual increase in the demand for pentamidine, a drug used to treat an extremely rare lung infection, was the HIV/AIDS epidemic first identified in 1981. Far from being a success, however, this discovery showed how inadequate global surveillance really was. As mentioned before, it is now known that the disease first emerged on a different continent about fifty years before it was first identified in San Francisco.

Surveillance capacity is weakest in developing countries; and failed, collapsed, and fragile states are the biggest challenge. The world is devoting an unprecedented amount of attention today to poliomyelitis because of the ongoing initiative to eradicate the disease, and yet surveillance has been inadequate. For example, polio was found in Sudan in 2004, three years after officials declared it had been eliminated. Subsequent analysis showed that the disease had remained endemic in the country all that time. If a disease that health officials are looking for cannot be identified, what are the chances that they will notice a disease that they do not even know exists?

Surveillance is also inadequate in rich countries. For example, an avian influenza virus (subtype H7N7) circulated undetected in the Dutch poultry industry for several months before a major outbreak occurred in 2003. Similarly, detection of BSE in the United Kingdom took longer than it should have. According to a formal inquiry into the BSE epidemic, farmers failed to refer BSE cases to the authorities at the early stage of the epidemic for fear that the discovery would harm them financially.

Reporting

Surveillance is of greatest benefit when new outbreaks are reported. It is the combination of surveillance and reporting that allows countries to take the steps necessary to protect their populations and to prevent the disease from spreading globally.

Unfortunately, perverse incentives work against fulfilling this need. Countries that report new outbreaks are typically "rewarded" by being made the targets of trade restrictions. Discovery of a single case of BSE, for example, routinely triggers a wholesale ban on beef imports from the country reporting the discovery—a restriction that can last a very long time.

The problem of reporting was dramatically and alarmingly demonstrated by the SARS outbreak. The World Health Organization first learned of a serious outbreak from unofficial sources, transmitted electronically and linked to its Global Outbreak Alert and Response Network. It was only the next day, a full three months after the epidemic started, that the Chinese government reported the SARS outbreak. Despite this failure, the SARS experience teaches that reporting is no longer the problem it once was. The availability of information from unofficial sources, coupled with the WHO's willingness to act on such information, means that countries gain less by hiding what they know and lose when their attempts at concealment are later exposed. The SARS experience has helped establish a new norm of behavior: the duty to report.

Response

The world's response to SARS may seem another source of comfort: the SARS outbreak did not become a pandemic. But SARS had characteristics that made control by the old-fashioned methods of quarantine and contact tracing easy. Persons with SARS showed symptoms, and became very ill, before they became infectious. Quarantine was thus effective in stopping transmission. And because the disease also had a lengthy incubation period, the people with whom infected persons had been in contact could be traced and isolated before they became ill and could infect others. Influenza has neither of these desirable properties and so is a much greater threat.

The incentives for the world to extinguish a disease at its source are strong, but the opportunity to do so depends on the other measures already noted—preparedness, surveillance, and reporting. These three areas, coupled with prevention, are the weakest links in the global system for addressing emerging infectious disease threats today.

International Health Regulations

None of these problems is new. Negotiation of trade rules in response to disease outbreaks began with the first international sanitary conference, hosted by France in 1851, and they continue today. Indeed, the agenda has barely shifted. One objective of the early conferences was to limit imports of disease into western Europe. The other was to standardize trade restrictions to block such imports. Recent negotiations to revise the International Health Regulations (IHR) focused on precisely the same issues.

The original purpose of the IHR, first established in 1951, was not only to "ensure the maximum security against the international spread of diseases," but to do so "with a minimum interference with world traffic." Unfortunately, the IHR failed to make much if any difference.

First, the IHR applied only to three diseases—cholera, plague, and yellow fever. China was under no legal obligation to notify the WHO of the SARS outbreak, even though its actions imperiled persons living in other countries. Second, compliance with the IHR was poor—partly because of the incentive not to report and partly because of the failure of the IHR to enforce compliance. Finally, the IHR failed to address the related incentive problems of underinvestment in surveillance. No country was obligated under the IHR to search for the first signs of the HIV/AIDS pandemic, for example.

Recent IHR revisions were meant to address these (and other) deficiencies, and they do mark a substantial shift. David Fidler, a leading expert on the subject, has called the revised IHR "one of the most radical and far-reaching changes in international law on public health since the beginning of international health cooperation in the mid-19th century."[1] Negotiations for these revisions went on for years, achieving nothing. Then SARS hit, and the WHO did all sorts of things it was not authorized to do, such as recommending that people not travel to at-risk areas like China and Toronto. The rest of the world, with the exception of the government of China and the mayor of Toronto, applauded. It was after this that the IHR were revised, mainly to give the WHO the authority to do what it had already done.

Scheduled to enter into force in May 2007 (for the countries that neither reject nor register reservations against them), the revised IHR contains a number of improvements. Three are most critical.

First, the revisions require notification of all "events that may constitute a public health emergency of international concern." These would include not only outbreaks of the three diseases listed in the current IHR, but of *all* diseases, including all newly emerging diseases.

Second, the revisions make reporting more reliable by allowing the WHO to take actions based on unofficial sources of information and by obligating countries to report outbreaks arising outside as well as inside their territories.

Third, the revisions require that any trade-related health measures adopted unilaterally be neither "more restrictive of international traffic" nor "more invasive or intrusive to persons than reasonably available alternatives that would achieve the appropriate level of health protection." Such measures must also be based on "scientific principles" and "available scientific evidence of a risk to human health." These measures make the revised IHR compatible with World Trade Organization (WTO) rules.

While all of these changes are welcome, the revisions will do little to address the fundamental weaknesses in the current system. The revisions require that nations "develop, strengthen and maintain . . . the capacity to detect, assess, notify and report" and "to respond promptly and effectively to public health threats and public health emergencies of international concern." But they do not provide the poorest countries with the means to deliver on this promise. Fundamentally, the IHR revisions fail to create *incentives* for countries to build a truly global surveillance and response capacity.

The IHR revisions can also be criticized on another level. They seek to address outbreaks but not the conditions that give rise to these outbreaks in the first place—conditions like poor sanitation, nutrition, and food safety, and the absence of minimum standards that can prevent resistant strains and dangerous mutations from emerging and spreading.

Emergence of a Global Response

As explained in a recent report by the U.S. Institute of Medicine, "infectious diseases are a global threat and therefore require a global response. . . . The United States' capacity to respond to microbial threats must therefore include a significant investment in the capacity of developing countries to monitor and address microbial threats as they arise."[2] The problem is that the incentives for the United States and other countries to make this investment on their own or by coordination only are weak. A multilateral effort is needed.

In January 2006 an international "pledging conference" on avian and human pandemic influenza was held in Beijing. The aim of the conference was to promote, mobilize, and coordinate financial support for a global response to the threat of an influenza pandemic. The organizers hoped to raise \$1.5 billion; in the event, \$1.9 billion was pledged. This would seem a victory for multilateralism, but the money pledged by the biggest donor, the United

States, represents less than 5 percent of the total U.S. budget for pandemic influenza. The balance of the spending is wrong.

A change in focus is also needed. Pandemic influenza is just one of many emerging infectious disease threats. As well, the U.S. response requires sustained, long-term investment, particularly in increasing capacity in developing countries.

Not all infectious diseases pose a global threat. Millions of people (children, mostly) in poor countries die every year of diseases that do not threaten people in rich countries. People living in rich countries are protected from these diseases, whether for reasons of geography, hygiene, sanitation, environmental modification, vector control, nutrition, or vaccination. This differential development has been propelled by, and has also reinforced, a domestic-oriented approach to public health. When a state can protect itself from infectious diseases, there is little need for it to cooperate with others. Public health becomes a matter of domestic policy and overseas development assistance.

The threat of emerging infectious diseases requires a different response. New diseases may arise anywhere and then spread, posing a risk to people everywhere. Existing institutional arrangements that emphasize defensive, national protection are an inadequate approach to this challenge. Shifting resources toward building a multilateral infrastructure will offer improved protection for every state.

The world is much better prepared than it was when SARS broke out in 2002. The IHR revisions, combined with the Sanitary and Phytosanitary Agreement of the WTO and an improved telecommunications infrastructure, mean that reporting is no longer the problem it once was. But a truly global approach is still lacking today, and this needs to change.

The problem at a fundamental level is underdevelopment. The conditions that give rise to new pathogens need to be dealt with directly: sanitation, hygiene, public health systems, farming practices, communication networks, and so on—this entire infrastructure is of global and not only local significance. Looked at from the perspective of emerging infectious diseases, the rich countries can gain directly from development of the poorest and weakest states, so they have reason to contribute more to that development. At the same time, these additional contributions must be linked to the meeting of global standards. Both are needed if the world is to be protected from the threat of emerging infectious diseases.

Part III

Forecasting

9

Ahead of the Curve: Anticipating Strategic Surprise

Peter Schwartz and Doug Randall

We live in a world of surprises. When they happen, the typical response is, "Who would have thought. . . ?" Who, for example, would have thought that Islamic terrorists would hijack airplanes and fly them into the World Trade Center and the Pentagon? That was a question that almost everyone—including senior military leaders of the United States—was asking after the fact. Yet, even the most devastating surprises are often inevitable. Many people did anticipate the terrorist attacks of September 11. During the last twenty years, a half-dozen well-known commissions predicted that something similar would occur: Terrorists would attack the World Trade Center again; airplanes could be used as weapons; Osama bin Laden would orchestrate attacks on symbols of U.S. power. Yet most Americans, as well as officials in both the Clinton and Bush administrations, focused their attention elsewhere while the inevitable grew imminent.

Why is the inevitable so often surprising? Many people blame a "failure of imagination." That is true, as statements go, but it does not get us closer to a solution. If a bunch of imaginative people are brought together in a room and asked to speculate about what might happen, they can easily create an abundance of wild scenarios. Even popular fiction can be ahead of the conjecture curve. Back in 1994 in *Debt of Honor,* novelist Tom Clancy wrote about a Japanese man who flew a 747 into the U.S. Capitol. No one reading that book argued that defense mechanisms should be set up to protect against crazed Japanese men; they saw this scenario as fiction and did not take it seriously.

The point is that imagining things is the easy part. What is hard is imagining future scenarios that are sufficiently believable to spur one to act in advance and find ways to persuade others to act. Achieving believability and action requires a depth of insight and understanding that is rare within companies or governments. This encompasses both an understanding of the world around the organization and deep insight into the mind-set of the decisionmakers within the organization.

Strategic Surprises

In advising major companies and governments on long-term issues, we at Global Business Network and the Monitor Group have come to see that the nature of surprise tends to be misunderstood. People mislabel many events as surprises, when they are actually inevitable and can be foreseen. More critically, people frequently focus on the wrong events altogether.

Instead of trying to react to all events and future scenarios equally, the challenge for leadership is to know which ones to act on. It is therefore essential to know how to identify, and then how to avoid, what we call strategic surprises.

A strategic surprise has three key elements that differentiate it from the run-of-the-mill surprises that are so common in today's complex world.

—It has an important impact on an organization or country.

—Because it challenges the conventional wisdom—"the official future," as we like to say—it is difficult to convince others to believe that the surprise is even possible.

—It is hard to imagine what can be done in response.

Strategic surprises, therefore, are those patterns of events that, if they were to occur, would make a big difference to the future, force decisionmakers to challenge their own assumptions of how the world works, and require hard choices today.

To be able to deal with strategic surprises, it is important to be aware of the two major traps into which people fall. First, decisionmakers tend to view sudden and significant shocks as most important when, in fact, they are not usually what matter most. Granted, the tsunami in Southeast Asia in December 2004 was a significant natural disaster. But simply because something momentous happens does not mean it is a strategic surprise.

Strategic surprises are game-changing events. They do not happen every year or even every decade. But when they take place, the rules of the game that were previously in place no longer apply. Strategic surprises usually reshape the rules of competition. The question then becomes: What are the assets needed to win, and when do strengths become weaknesses, and vice versa? Vantage point also matters; something can be a strategic surprise for one company or country but for not another, because an event's impact may be felt differently.

Second, the myth about strategic surprise is that the surprise is difficult to identify. Yet, if big uncertainties in the world around us are recognized and explored, important phenomena can often be seen—and monitored—as they emerge. It is easier for people to imagine how they might deal with a danger they recognize, even slightly, than one that comes out of left field. This, in turn, heightens their ability to act or persuade others to act.

The sudden collapse of the Soviet Union in 1991 is one of the great strategic surprises of the twentieth century. It fits the definition of a strategic surprise because it made a huge difference to global politics and economics, it challenged the conventional wisdom that the Soviet Union would exist forever, and it was difficult to imagine how anyone could prepare a response to such a radically new world. Although it was a "surprise" that had been foreseen well in advance, most people did not act.

These are lessons that one of us, Peter Schwartz, learned firsthand as the scenario planner who helped Royal Dutch/Shell successfully anticipate the developments of the early 1980s in the Soviet Union, and then respond appropriately. The first hints that something was happening arose nearly a decade earlier when Peter, then at SRI International, engaged in an ongoing exchange program with a group of Soviet writers, poets, economists, and other leading-edge thinkers who were exploring the cultural, economic, and political evolution of their society. At that time, they were already asking questions about the tensions simmering beneath the surface of the Soviet Union's socialist façade. Despite seeing the fault lines, none of these people could construct a plausible scenario in which the cold war wound down before 2025.

Peter later left SRI to lead Royal Dutch/Shell's famed scenario planning team in the 1980s. At the time, Shell was one of the largest holders of oil reserves in the world. But it faced growing competition for access to new resources from state oil companies in such countries as Brazil, Mexico, and Norway. The areas in the world where a private company could explore for oil were shrinking, so Shell needed to imagine the future of oil and how the landscape could change over the long term to create new opportunities.

Peter decided to study both Mexico and the Soviet Union, which were then off-limits to foreign private companies. Shell knew something about both countries, having been thrown out of them by hostile governments in the 1920s, and perceived that meaningful opportunities might one day reemerge because of changing geopolitics. The research into Mexico, while interesting, was a dry hole. But what the group learned about the Soviet Union proved fascinating and critical. During the early 1980s, the Soviet Union was proposing to build a pipeline to bring its plentiful natural gas resources to the European market. Shell owned a competing natural gas field in Norway, but it was under 1,500 feet of water. (And at $9 billion, it proved to be the most expensive platform ever built.) Natural gas from that field was four times as costly as Soviet supplies.

At the time, the Americans and Europeans debated whether a Soviet pipeline would give Moscow strategic leverage over Europe (which is what has transpired today). Western European leaders wondered whether their "enemies" should pay a hefty premium to exploit strategically invulnerable natural resources. In effect, Shell had a pressing need to understand if there was a plausible scenario in which the cold war ended and the Soviet Union stopped being a real strategic concern.

Shell's planning group did a tremendous amount of research. It studied the experience of Hungary, then transitioning toward capitalism as a model of "goulash communism." This country was an indicator that things could change rapidly in the Soviet sphere. Shell also had access to a wealth of data about Soviet energy consumption. But when Peter's team compared those data with the best available information about economic output, it realized that the pictures did not match: the amount of energy being used was insufficient for the stated level of economic output. Either the energy data were wrong, or the Soviets were much more energy-efficient than anyone imagined, or the output data were wrong. It turned out that the energy data were correct. This discovery was an important signal that the Soviet Union was already beginning to collapse under the weight of its own economic contradictions. The only question was what the postcollapse environment would look like.

When Peter presented these findings to Shell's board of directors in 1984, the idea that the Soviet Union would soon collapse seemed thoroughly implausible. Although President Ronald Reagan talked incessantly about America's long-term battle with the Evil Empire, people within Shell (and within the U.S. government) had trouble believing collapse was possible. Even if it was, they did not know what they could do about it. Fortunately, the Shell scenario team had also identified the key indicators that would signal which scenario was unfolding, and over the next eighteen months, all the "collapse" indicators flashed. As history proved, the group got the scenario right for the right reasons. It was a true strategic surprise: an important set of issues, decisions, and results that fundamentally influenced future actions.

The demise of the Soviet Union was not that difficult to foresee, however. George Kennan had predicted it in his influential essay on containment in 1947.[1] What *was* difficult was convincing Shell's board of directors that collapse was possible and then to take action, even as, one by one, the indicators turned positive. Ultimately, Shell was able to profit from that call: it was the first major Western company to realign its exploration strategies around the new realities of what soon would be called the "former Soviet Union."

How to Sense Strategic Surprises

We live in a society that relies heavily on precise predictions. Pundits who do not make predictions—or who make predictions that are not exactly right—lose credibility. However, thinking about the future and about strategic surprise is a messy business for which precise predictions are the wrong concept. The goal is not more accurate predictions. Rather, it is better decisions and more effective action.

Instead of claiming that anyone can *predict* what is going to happen, we argue that everyone, from analysts to decisionmakers, can see the forces as they are taking shape and not be blindsided when those changes inevitably reshape the global environment. Anticipating strategic surprise gives decisionmakers the ability to look in the right place for game-changing events and to track them systematically. As these scenarios become more plausible, and ever more imminent, decisionmakers can then pay attention to the right things when they matter most. This kind of insight leads to better questions rather than better answers, but better questions are very, very important.

At this point, some people might say that only specialized consultants, or remarkable companies with access to unique information, can anticipate significant future events. Not so: anyone can sense these forces if they make it a priority and are committed to a systematic approach. Poorly structured, ill-defined, difficult-to-grasp problems can be solved. They are not intractable. They just require novel thinking and approaches.

So how do ordinary people and organizations sense strategic surprises in practice? We have found it useful to construct a portfolio of approaches.

BEING IMAGINATIVE AND SYSTEMATIC

Structurally, organizations must embed two fundamentally different and intersecting orientations—being *imaginative* and being *systematic*. This is a *both/and*, not an *either/or*, approach. One cannot foresee strategic surprises without being imaginative, but the results will not be believable without being systematic.

It is critical to push people's imagination out to the very edges of believability to see the full range of the possible. Ideas that may be on the fringe now often have a way of entering the mainstream. One scenario that seemed relegated to science-fiction movies a decade ago was that of an asteroid hitting the earth. Today, the United Nations is meeting on the subject and the National Aeronautics and Space Administration is taking the possibility seriously.

It is also important to look for events that seem to have a low probability of happening but that would have a high impact were they to occur. In mathematics, the probability of a large number of events concatenating into a single story—that is, any given scenario—is vanishingly small. But when one considers something as large and complex as a nation or a city or a large company, many low-probability, high-impact events become possible. If there are 1,000 such events and the probability of each one happening is 1 in 100,000, then there is a pretty good chance 1 will occur, and fairly soon.

To encourage imaginative thinking, our company brings leaders out of their element—and their comfort zone. We expose them to different organizations and environments through "learning journeys." We hold meetings atop tall buildings with plenty of windows to inspire the long view. We encourage people to role-play belief systems they do not endorse so they can see the other side of an issue and to experiment with improvisation as a tool for responding to the unexpected.

In this case, it helps to live where ideas are a key currency, as they are in the San Francisco Bay Area. By being exposed to many new ideas first, Californians have a strong track record of taking thinking that seems implausible and making it real. New ideas from California have a slightly higher degree of credibility than those coming from many other parts of the world. That is not trivial.

Being systematic is equally critical and means exploring, in a rigorous way, how significant events might unfold. Can one construct a plausible, rigorous pathway from here to there? If so, then the event has to be taken seriously. It is fashionable right now to say that practically anything that pops up on someone's radar screen is an unforeseeable, "emergent" phenomenon. People say that surprises *emerge*, meaning that they surface without any warning, so leaders therefore have no ability to identify surprises ahead of time. This is mainly an excuse for a lack of discipline in systematically collecting and analyzing information. Senior managers and officials *can* anticipate events, and pretending that they are not discoverable is analytical laziness. It means these leaders either did not go through a disciplined process to surface the unexpected, or they failed to adequately analyze and communicate the surprises so that people believed in and acted on them.

There is also a tendency in organizations to rush to an opinion. The president, for example, wants to know *right now* if a country has weapons of mass destruction. Incomplete information is unacceptable. Few organizations reward those who are able to say, "I don't know" and "I need more data on such and such points."

Being systematic at both the human and organizational levels makes it easier to build systems to detect surprises even with highly imperfect data. Decisionmakers can act with less information or with information that comes in over months and years. Policymakers can take a "real options" view of problems in which new information changes the confidence in or the direction of their decisions as it emerges, causing them to adapt and act differently.

THE FILTERS APPROACH

One relevant metaphor for collecting information is "filters." Organizations need multiple filters, each one measuring different kinds of information at different granularities. This is similar to building filters to measure sunlight, air particles, or ultrasonic waves. A multiplicity of frameworks, perspectives, and experiences is needed, each surfacing different kinds and categories of insight into the baseline information, many of which overlap.

Most organizations focus on a single source of data when looking to the future. In fact, corporate research departments often separate competitive, market, industry, and financial research; likewise, government intelligence organizations are divided according to source: human (HUMINT), signals (SIGINT), photographic, open source (OSINT), and other types of intelligence. Such organizational structures may simplify data collection but can also make processing good insights more difficult.

There are alternatives. Structured databases can capture and relate varied information like data on demographics, economics, and energy use. Information markets can help make sense of the "wisdom of crowds." Analyst reports can target underlying, quantifiable trends. In many situations, from national security to corporate competitive intelligence, secret information is often valued over publicly available or open-source information, which may be marginalized or ignored altogether. A portfolio theory of collecting information, however, emphasizes using a multiplicity of data sources—both public and private. But the integration of all that disparate information ultimately relies upon the intuitive judgments of the human mind.

In an interview with us, James Surowiecki, *New Yorker* business columnist and author of *The Wisdom of Crowds*, noted three open-source ways to find relevant data and opinions outside of one's most familiar frame of reference: discover unfamiliar terrain on the Internet; take high-quality but undervalued academic work and transport it to a different environment where it can be of high value; and read outside your field of expertise to find potentially useful metaphors and conceptual insights.[2] When multiple sources are used and interpreted together, we have found that it is easier to separate the signal from the noise.

In our work, we have also taken the relatively rare step of creating and tapping networks of thoughtful people who have their fingers on the pulse of change. We talk regularly to these artists, scientists, innovators, writers, and politicians to listen for clues about important trends. And we urge organizations to reach out to individuals from multiple disciplines who think differently and use a variety of filters to make sense of information. For example, the Global Business Network team that is working on security and intelligence issues includes a neuroscientist, a political scientist, an intellectual historian, an MBA, and a former intelligence analyst. We supplement that team with a network of insightful, external people to ensure cross-disciplinary thinking and varied perspectives. Of course, it is less efficient to manage so much diversity, which is why so many organizations don't do it. But avoiding strategic surprise is not about efficiency.

Similarly, getting out of the office and experiencing issues firsthand also is critical. Anyone who visits Shanghai, for example, will find it hard to deny that China is going to shake the world in the next fifty years. Reading articles about China pales in comparison to the visceral experience of being there.

PROCESSING INFORMATION DIFFERENTLY

Instead of simply looking at how information is *collected*, it is critical to think about how information from multiple filters is *processed* effectively. People who operate in a secret world, as intelligence agencies do, need to ask how to find and process information in a public environment without giving away secrets. Those who operate in the business world must move beyond a narrow reliance on market research departments to uncover what is really going on. In both situations, leaders need insightful ways of imagining how collected data come together and how to think about the choices that arise from that integration.

We use many frameworks for processing information. One is STEEP, which stands for the social, technological, environmental, economic, and political forces that compose the key drivers of change in the business environment.

Another is "scenario thinking," which involves developing a two-by-two matrix that juxtaposes the most important critical uncertainties facing an organization. This provides a framework for imagining four different, plausible, and challenging futures against which strategies and choices can be developed and tested. "Choice structuring" is a framework that requires people to identify clearly the options they face, the influences on their decisions, and the data required to make those decisions. Many other information-processing frameworks exist; the most important lesson is not to use a single interpretative approach.

Another tempting, but counterproductive, tendency is adherence to a comprehensive "theory of the case." Consciously or unconsciously, people often form a theory of how geopolitics, economics, or the dynamics of an industry or technology works. This is a powerful source of systematic blindness. In finance, modern portfolio theory cautions against investing all your money in one stock; so why would you want to invest all your strategic thinking in one theory? In the 1980s this was a big reason why many people missed the obvious signs of the Soviet Union's coming collapse.

Some individuals think they can get around this blind spot by having multiple theories, or, in the language of investing, by diversifying their assets. While several theories are better than one, the risk of being blindsided remains high, precisely because strategic surprises tend to fall through the cracks between the theories.

LOOKING OUTSIDE-IN AND INSIDE-OUT

In our work, we follow a systematic way of surfacing surprises. We rigorously construct a range of plausible scenarios about the future that enables leaders to explore and exploit the unknown and take action in the face of uncertainty. To do that, we look at a problem from two perspectives: outside-in and inside-out.

An outside-in perspective means systematically exploring the major forces of change: demographic, social, technological, economic, environmental, political. For example, one might analyze immigration patterns, new developments in telecommunications technologies, shifting geopolitical relationships, income disparities, and so on. By studying in depth these trends and the interactions between them, it is possible to identify the forces that are likely to produce a big discontinuity in the future and its relevance to the organization.

In thinking about strategic surprise from this perspective, it is important not to focus simply on events themselves, but rather on the contexts within which they are developing. For instance, the game-changing potential of the

Yom Kippur War in 1973 would have been radically different without the larger context of the cold war. Understanding these contexts then becomes part of the analytical process of anticipating surprise.

The next step is to take an inside-out approach. Here, the question is less about what is going on outside in the world, but rather: What are the risks to the organization? What are the key elements of vulnerability? What would make a big difference in the future? For oil companies, the significant issues might include the price of oil, access to exploration opportunities, or environmental regulations. By pushing those elements to the extreme, new insights emerge: What happens if oil prices skyrocket or plummet? What difference would it make? What if access to new exploration opportunities is denied or assets are nationalized? How could that happen?

When Peter worked at Shell in the early 1980s, he used this approach to develop scenarios about the future price of oil. In a situation much like today, oil had reached \$70 a barrel (in 2006 dollars), and the big strategic issue facing oil companies was how to deal with the "cash mountain" that would result if oil hit \$120 a barrel. In that case the entire industry would struggle to reinvest its enormous profits and diversify into other industries, because oil would start running out by the mid-1990s.

Instead, Shell asked, "Is there any way the price of oil could go in precisely the opposite direction?" The planning group constructed three scenarios, with oil priced at \$120, \$70, and \$16 a barrel. Not surprisingly, Shell's managing directors quite liked the first two scenarios and thought the third highly unlikely. That scenario showed what would happen if oil started behaving just like any other commodity—according to the laws of supply and demand. When the price went up, people would drive less and use less oil; simultaneously, companies would try to cash in on high prices by producing more oil from more expensive sources. The strategy team had developed the indicators that would tell the company which scenario was playing out, and the board had the foresight to allow them to track these signals. Sure enough, by the summer of 1985 the indicators were clearly pointing to a looming price collapse. Shell was able to profit from the downturn by buying oil fields for far less than their owners had originally paid and by trading oil against companies that failed to imagine just how low the price of oil could go.

The key point was not that this group of people predicted exactly *when* the price of oil would collapse, but rather that it understood *how* the price might collapse and *which* long-term indicators to watch. The company's directors did not have to accept or reject the scenario on day one but rather could adapt to the indicators over time. They were therefore better prepared and avoided some big mistakes, such as buying fields or companies when oil was priced at $70 a barrel.

MAKING SURPRISE BELIEVABLE

There is a tendency to deny strategic surprises altogether. For example, people say, "China can't maintain its recent success, can it?" And yet China keeps growing in importance.

Much of the reluctance to grapple with such game-changing issues stems from an unwillingness to face the consequences of taking different scenarios seriously. Those consequences might interfere with long-held mental models, organizational structures, or self- or business interests.

Denial is a powerful form of cognitive bias and one of the most common reactions found in organizations of all sizes. Denial is the failure to believe or acknowledge that an organization is facing uncertainty and may need to make major changes to respond and adapt. Denial can stifle creativity and make companies and nations susceptible to strategic surprise.

An example from our own experience concerns the rise of religious politics in the United States. One of the big changes of the last two decades has been the growth and political influence of the fundamentalist Right. This game-changing phenomenon was foreseen in a 2000 book by Robert William Fogel, and before that in sociologist Robert Bellah's extensive writings on religion in America.[3] In his book, Fogel argued that the United States was going through yet another religious revival, this time partially driven by rising birthrates among fundamentalists (and low birthrates among nonfundamentalists). Even though a colleague urged us to read Fogel's book, insisting that this trend was critical, several of us completely ignored it. We were in denial about the implications of a religiously conservative America, and this competing perspective conflicted with our established mental models. We therefore missed out on alerting our clients to an important force in American culture and politics.

Because denial is such a strong influence, one of the most important steps in constructing an imaginative and systematic analysis of the future involves making the analysis believable. For starters, this requires bringing the portfolio of analytical approaches together to create scenarios that could produce significant surprises. Well-crafted scenarios can help organizations that suffer from denial about future change to rehearse it in advance. By articulating challenging, yet plausible, ways in which the future could evolve, scenarios encourage management teams to "think the unthinkable," anticipate surprises, and try out new possibilities. In scenario exercises, we encourage teams to explore the strategies they would pursue under radically different scenarios or external circumstances.

Scenario-thinking exercises generally begin with a rigorous fact-finding phase, where the "official future" is articulated. Rather than conducting research about how a company is performing, or what the future is likely to be, the research builds a story describing the assumptions that management has about the future, based on interviews and observable actions.

When our team presents the threat or opportunity of a strategic surprise to clients, we spend a lot of time telling such stories. Constructing good scenarios involves understanding the decisionmakers and how they process information; knowing their mind-set, what they perceive to be the risks ahead, and where they are confident about the future; developing a theory of change for them; choosing the words and graphics that will have an emotional impact; and figuring out how they need to hear the story in order to act. Articulating the *official future* is one way to show people the need to believe in *another* future, which sets the groundwork for believing in *alternative* futures. And narratives—stories, with characters, plots, and paths—help to make these futures real.

In 2003 we constructed a scenario about climate change for the Pentagon that received a great deal of press attention.[4] We did not invent the story, however. We got our facts from a National Academy of Sciences report entitled "Abrupt Climate Change: Inevitable Surprises." What we did was construct a worst-case scenario that was *believable* during a time when many were still skeptical that sudden cooling could result from global warming. We did that by explaining the science in a way anyone could understand and then tying the data to a hypothesis about the huge impacts from climate change. We also based it on a real event that happened 8,200 years ago—when the climate cooled suddenly after a period of gradual warming—as proof that it was possible.

When we began to develop our scenario, the collective, conventional wisdom was that the world was facing a gradual rise in global warming that would take hundreds of years to play out. Policymakers would have plenty of time to take counteractions, such as those laid out in the Kyoto Protocol. The time frames for both the problem and the solutions were being measured in centuries.

Mental models are misleading, however. The average temperature may be rising gradually but, as they say, you can drown in a river of averages. (The average depth of the Rio Grande might make it safe to cross, but you can certainly drown where the river is deepest.) Likewise, the average climate of the world may indeed change gradually, but scientists know now that when energy in the atmosphere increases and the relationship of the ocean to the atmosphere is altered, the results will be more extreme, not more average. The world will experience more hurricanes and droughts, more extremes of hot and cold, faster rises in the sea level.

All the warning signs we developed decades ago in our early work on climate change, and have been carefully tracking ever since, have pointed increasingly to the fact that the world is in a period of rapid and dramatic change. The early signals are apparent right now: the slowdown of the northward movement of the Gulf Stream; the ultra-rapid melting of the polar ice cap; and the disruption of the salmon season off the West coast of the United States, which has been attributed to the failure of nutrients in the lower depths of the Pacific Ocean to rise to the levels in which the salmon swim.

The Earth is clearly in a time of rapid rather than gradual climate change, and clear signs of environmental catastrophe will be evident in a few decades, not centuries. The most visible marker of this new era will occur when the nation of Bangladesh disappears from the planet—a catastrophe that will happen sooner than people think. Rather than sea levels rising to destroy it, Bangladesh will first see storm surges that regularly flood most of the country, affecting three out of four Bangladeshis (compared with one in four today) and making the entire country basically uninhabitable.

The fundamental, game-changing question then becomes: Is this a process of slow adaptation and mitigation in a world that is gradually warming, or an urgent crisis in which climate extremes will soon dramatically transform continents and countries? The first scenario might lead a country to forgo nuclear power as an alternative source to carbon-based energy sources, while the second might make nuclear power an urgent priority. There are real consequences to these perceptions. It was precisely this shift in perceptions that led British prime minister Tony Blair to alter his stance on nuclear power from firmly opposed to reluctantly supportive.

Generally speaking, scientists do not present their information so dramatically—and neither do many intelligence or corporate analysts. But telling the story of abrupt climate change like this brought the immediacy and impacts of global warming to life. Interestingly, a few months after our report was published, the movie *The Day after Tomorrow* came out. It told a similar tale in an even more imaginative, if less accurate, way. The result? It made our report look moderate, and today, the impact of abrupt climate change is moving to the center of the scientific and political agendas.

Preparing for Future Surprises

Anticipating strategic surprise is ultimately valuable in terms of preparedness. Organizations that have thought about such significant issues are much more likely to discern important, emerging trends early on; identify the indicators that tell them something big is happening; and put in place the sensors to detect strategic surprise as it unfolds. If the key indicators are getting worse, the worst-case scenario becomes more and more plausible.

This in turn gives organizations the ability to act in advance if they believe a particular scenario is unfolding. It gives them more maneuvering room and time to create new options. The more powerful an organization or country is, the more important early recognition and anticipatory action become. The stakes get that much higher, and the probability of getting surprised becomes even more likely. Such preparedness results in the ability to seize opportunities, such as gaining first-mover advantage when surprise happens, and to deal more effectively with threats, such as minimizing risks with contingency plans or even preventing certain events from happening.

In our daily work, we are constantly engaged with major companies and organizations, talking with leading-edge thinkers, traveling the world, and using the important tools mentioned here to scan the landscape for "what's next." Global Business Network has been in business for nearly twenty years because our clients highly value the insights such methods produce. And while we are not without our mistakes, we have managed to anticipate many of the major strategic surprises of the past two decades and get others to take action.

We can already see on the horizon the signals of scenarios that may seem implausible now but which would be game-changing if they were to occur. Whether they happen in exactly the way outlined below is not important. What is critical is developing the right indicators and responding if they do.

The Breakup of Indonesia. Two powerful dictators held Indonesia together for decades after it achieved independence from the Netherlands: Sukarno from 1945 to 1967; and Suharto from 1967 to 1998. When Suharto's government toppled after a massive public uprising, the possibility of breakup became increasingly likely. While Aceh appears to be calm, for now, after thirty years of separatist battles and the devastating December 2004 tsunami, East Timor has been the site of massive unrest after breaking away from Indonesia, Java has been rocked by a major earthquake, Sumatra has experienced a huge outbreak of bird flu, and Islamic fundamentalists have been waging war against Indonesia's secular society. And despite recent evidence of an economic recovery, even after large cuts in domestic oil subsidies, for various reasons oil-rich Indonesia is no longer a major oil exporter. Economic and political conditions are changing dramatically, and the situation is ripe to explode, with large consequences for the entire region. Imagine a dozen East Timors.

The Rise of Quantum Computing. Many people believe that we will run out of computing breakthroughs in the not-too-distant future, and that Moore's

Law of ever-multiplying computing power will reach the natural limits of silicon chips and ordinary physics. Conversely, over the next fifteen to twenty years, the world will see the rise of quantum computing, which harnesses the unique new capabilities of quantum physics to revolutionize computing. It will free computers from the limits of the binary numbers one and zero, and allow many states to coexist simultaneously. Quantum computing will be used to solve entirely new scientific problems, and it will change the rules of the game. It could enable entirely new inventions, such as the ability to understand and control how proteins shape the development of the body, while also producing new sources of value and business models.

The Collapse of NATO. Many observers think the North Atlantic Treaty Organization will persist, but we think it appears virtually certain to disappear within a decade. The fundamental interests of the United States and Europe, NATO's key powers, are diverging. The Americans will no longer want to pay billions of dollars to protect rich countries like France and Germany. As postimperial powers, the Europeans are reluctant to get involved in peacekeeping missions in places like Bosnia and Darfur. Their goal instead will be containing U.S. power. Most U.S. forces are already out of continental Europe (with a small increase at NATO's far eastern border). The United Kingdom remains suspicious of the continental Europeans and is likely to side with the United States in this split.

A Grand European-Russian Alliance. As the strategic interests of Europe and the United States diverge, Russia is increasingly likely to get itself into deep economic trouble. When this happens, Europe could come to its aid, offering money, markets, talent, and technology in exchange for access to Russia's abundant natural gas, oil, and timber resources. More important, it could gain strategic strength from Russia's 10,000 nuclear missiles. An alliance could produce a global superpower that rivals the United States and China in military and economic strength. This scenario could be triggered by a demographic collapse in Russia. The dramatic decline in the birthrate years ago, combined with a sharp fall in life expectancy among working-age men, will cause the Russian labor force to slip into a steady decline. This will in turn lead to an economic collapse in the years ahead. Only high oil prices are protecting the economy now.

The Breakdown of the Euro and the EU. A countervailing force in Europe could also take place as the continent's much-heralded economic and political integration begins to fall apart at the seams. Important indicators of this scenario have already occurred. The rejection of the European Constitution by France and the Netherlands dealt the project of political integration a major setback that will last for years. The idea that the European Union will become a federal system is off the table politically. Equally vulnerable is the euro project. The key economies of France, Germany, and Italy have significantly diverged in terms of budget deficits, inflation rates, and growth rates. Italy is desperate to get out of the euro and to revalue its currency, a habitual fiscal lever in the past. Political and economic integration reinforce each other. If the various forms of union are to succeed, they must proceed together. If they both retreat together, it may be difficult to sustain the entire European project. While it is just as likely that this scenario may not happen, for the first time observers can actually consider this possibility and look for the indicators.

Egypt Goes Fundamentalist. The signals are obvious: A dictatorial leader is grooming his son to rule after him; a corrupt elite is running a country with a rapidly growing population; a small but aggressively violent elite tries to seize power. What does this scenario sound like? Iran in 1978. It obviously will not happen in exactly the same way. But what if elections are held and the fundamentalists win? Will the situation look like Algeria in 1992, when a fundamentalist victory was suppressed, leading to a decade of civil war? So far, most of the world is not focused on the growing likelihood of this scenario.

An Anti-American World. Suppose the rise of populist governments in Latin America is an early indicator of a global swing to the political Left, driven by inequality. Previous decades have been dominated by the United States, markets, and democracy. Imagine that the more socialist countries like China, France, and Russia are the models for the decades ahead, not the pure capitalists of the United States and Britain. Global anti-Americanism, increased regulation, a decline in market integration, and a rise in protectionism could all trigger a huge global downturn. Globalization could unravel into competing mercantilist systems jockeying with the United States for global supremacy. China is already showing signs of creating an economic alliance across Asia and the developing world in the scramble to lock up natural resources. Russian market reforms are at best spotty, at worst disintegrating. Could all of these countries converge in a new era of containment with the United States as the nation to be contained?

Each of these scenarios is beginning to exhibit all the hallmarks of a strategic surprise. The warning signs are there if one's eyes are open to them. Whether or not they come true in exactly the ways outlined here, the world's business and government leaders will be immeasurably better off if they carefully consider how these scenarios could come to pass and act today to create maneuvering room for the radically different world that these game-changing events could create.

10

Can Scenarios Help Policymakers Be Both Bold and Careful?

Robert Lempert

Surprise, of both good and bad varieties, has become a ubiquitous feature of the world facing American policymakers. Leaders have come to expect adverse surprises, from terrorist attacks to global pandemics to signs that global warming is emerging faster than previously imagined. But many of the most serious, festering problems facing the United States—from encouraging a free, just, and stable global order to ensuring that the American middle class can thrive in a globalized world—also require leaders who can transform some of what seem like today's inexorable trends. The need to nurture beneficial yet seemingly unlikely change, while avoiding a Pandora's box of unintended consequences, poses a difficult challenge. American policymakers must, paradoxically, be both bold and careful.

A bold policy seeks to create a future very different from the present. A careful policy guards against the consequences when plans inevitably go awry. The last few years provide a rich case study of bold U.S. policymakers who failed to be careful. For instance, the architects of the Iraq war recognized that the then-current situation in the Middle East was unsustainable. But in trying to remake Iraq, they fell victim to adverse events they refused to imagine. Future policymakers must not only manage the direct consequences of these costly initiatives; they may face an electorate grown more dubious about grand projects and large visions altogether. America still wields great power, but future leaders may find it difficult to justify bold policies even when they are most needed.

Can scenarios help American policymakers attain the paradoxical balance between boldness and care? Increasingly popular in business and government, scenarios are carefully constructed stories about the future intended to help people make better decisions in the face of uncertainty. Scenarios often come in groups that illuminate how the future might play out if key unanticipated events break one way or another. What would the future be like if oil prices keep rising, or if they once again decline? What would the daily news bring in a world with nuclear-armed, Islamist governments who felt undeterred, or in a world where the U.S. market responded to higher gas taxes with quick deployment of low-cost, petroleum-free automobile technology? Well-crafted scenarios help people, in the words of scenario master Pierre Wack, by changing their "assumptions about how the world works and compelling them to reorganize their mental models of reality."[1]

At their best, scenarios can often help decisionmakers overcome the psychological and organizational barriers that make it difficult to manage surprise. But when produced by committees or tendered for broad public debate, scenarios rarely achieve this goal. The notion of surprise is rooted in expectations. A surprise may or may not be unlikely, but it is certainly a change not widely expected. Scenarios aim to address surprise by strategically expanding the diversity of futures people consider. This is not easy to do, because humans have a deep psychological aversion to ambiguity. They crave to know more about the future than they ever can and thus often place too much confidence in some futures and pay too little attention to others. No group can consider more than a small number of scenarios, and when generated by committees, the safe or expected can crowd out the most important.

Scenario masters such as Wack and his most famous student, Peter Schwartz, working with a small group of clients they know well, can often find a succinct set of scenarios that focus attention on key opportunities and dangers. New information technology may help turn this scenario art into a more systematic method, provide the means for even committees and bureaucracies to deliberately justify the choice of a small number of the most important scenarios, and thus make it easier for Americans to demand that their leaders be both bold and careful.

Imaging a Multiplicity of Futures

Psychologist Jon Baron at the University of Pennsylvania conducted an experiment that captures how aversion to ambiguity can affect decisions. Baron assembled two groups of students with diverse opinions about how the United

States ought to respond to climate change. He then presented each group with the United Nations' summary of the scientific consensus regarding the climate change threat. One group received only the scientists' best-estimate forecasts; the other, both the forecasts and a description of the large uncertainties involved. Those given only the forecasts quickly agreed the United States ought to act. But those also given the uncertainties hardened in their initial, disparate views and reached no consensus on steps forward. Baron's experiment illustrates that people generally want a sense of certainty before acting.

This aversion to ambiguity, well established in the psychological literature, is not lost on policymakers. Those who reach leadership positions in government and business have a clear bias toward optimism and confidence. They see risk as a challenge to be overcome through skill and determination; they tend to downplay risks they cannot control; and they understand that a display of confidence makes it more likely they will achieve their goals. In his study of how senior U.S. officials use intelligence, Greg Treverton, former vice chair of the National Intelligence Council, describes a process he calls *overarguing.*[2] Senior decisionmakers communicate with one another, their organizations, and the public by using narratives—stories that combine statements of goals, assumptions about the world, and plans for action. When they craft these narratives, policymakers strive to appear more certain than they actually are, knowing full well that a storyline acknowledging their underlying uncertainty would undercut their authority in policy debates.

This tendency to overargue may prove most dangerous when decisionmakers have their greatest opportunity to affect the future. It is easy now to make fun of a Bush administration official's boast rejecting "reality-constrained" thinkers in favor of those who understood America's power to create its own future.[3] But the official did touch on an element of truth. Human societies can find themselves poised near tipping points, those dramatic moments where a small push may nudge events along a fundamentally new path.

When the world lies far from such tipping points, the future is largely predictable because it will inexorably follow current trends regardless of actions taken by policymakers or anybody else. But near such points, well-timed and skillful actions can reverse established trends and set events on a new course. For instance, in the late 1950s and early 1960s, American civil rights leaders captured a moment with a new concept—that the statement "all men are created equal" really meant *all*—and with new legislation that placed U.S. race relations on a fundamentally new, if yet incomplete, path.

Yet tipping points become certain only once they have been crossed, so that times of great opportunity also present great ambiguity. Management guru

Peter Drucker described discontinuities as "the shapers of tomorrow's society," "the unsuspected and apparently insignificant [that] derail the massive and seemingly invincible trends of today."[4] Good leaders are often among the first to note the future promise in seemingly inconsequential developments. But most apparently insignificant trends remain that way, even when policymakers work hard to make them grow into a dominant force.

Leaders who rise to the top of large organizations have good reason to trust that their judgment and confidence will serve them well when they face a familiar world that matches their instincts and experience. But in grappling with a novel future, the narratives that people find most resonant may no longer describe the world in which they live. Aversion to ambiguity can make it hard for leaders and their organizations to focus on the combination of surprises that best allows them to both exploit new opportunities and manage unintended consequences. They may miss opportunities for bold action because they underestimate their ability to shape fluid events; they may be surprised because they fail to see signs the world has changed; or they may boldly bet on the wrong future, wasting their nation's blood and treasure trying to exploit a tipping point that will not tip.

Scenarios aim to overcome these problems by making it easier for decisionmakers to imagine a multiplicity of plausible futures. In the 1960s, futurist Herman Kahn first appropriated the Hollywood term *scenarios* to describe the stories he devised to help people think more seriously about the "unthinkable" consequences of a nuclear war. Today scenarios help their audiences embrace ambiguity by suspending disbelief, encouraging them to imagine the consequences of an often unwelcome or seemingly implausible future without requiring them to believe that future is likely to happen.

To choose the best small number of scenarios to consider, scenario practice begins with the challenge facing the decisionmakers, ranks the most significant driving forces according to their level of uncertainty and their impact on trends seemingly relevant to that decision, and then creates a handful of scenarios that explore different manifestations of those driving forces. For instance, how long should the United States keep its troops in Iraq? A set of scenarios designed to inform that question might include futures where only the extended presence of American forces can provide the security needed to restrain the violence, as well as futures where the American presence mainly prolongs the conflict. Such scenarios might help decisionmakers assess policies while holding in their heads two important and contradictory views of the future.

Limits to Traditional Scenarios

In 1940, future general Matthew Ridgway wrote a war-game scenario about a surprise attack on the U.S. fleet at Pearl Harbor. Ridgway's fellow officers refused to play out the war game because they regarded it as a "possibility so improbable that it did not constitute a proper basis for maneuver."[5] Little is different today. Creative people can always suggest provocative scenarios. But to get anything done, serious organizations need mechanisms and procedures to sift through the chaff and focus on the most important futures. Yet with so many possible scenarios to consider, it becomes easy for an organization to sweep away the important in favor of the convenient. Novel, unverifiable, or inopportune events perceived as low probability can quickly become zero probability and are dropped from the debate.

This process is well illustrated by recent attempts to create greenhouse gas emissions scenarios that would help governments devise effective strategies for addressing the threat of global climate change. The leaders of the United States and other countries recognize that human combustion of fossil fuels has significantly increased the atmosphere's concentrations of greenhouse gases such as carbon dioxide and begun to change the earth's climate. They must make difficult decisions about how, and how extensively, to regulate such pollution; what new emissions-reducing technologies to develop; and how to help farmers, coastal communities, and other vulnerable parts of society adapt to coming changes. To help inform these debates, scientists, economists, and other scholars concerned with climate change have created a variety of greenhouse gas emissions scenarios for the twenty-first century. The most impressive and authoritative effort has been the Special Report on Emissions Scenarios (SRES) sponsored by the United Nations' Intergovernmental Panel on Climate Change (IPCC).[6] The creators of these scenarios worked hard to implement the approach practiced by Wack and Schwartz but fell far short of results that can help national governments seize the opportunities and avoid the dangers related to climate change.

To assess the SRES effort, it is important to note the extent to which climate change presents a challenge of competing surprises. In one plausible future, greenhouse gas emissions will continue rising and the earth's natural environment will change more rapidly and dramatically than anything in recorded human experience. Already, as thinning ice caps and glaciers provide the first, gripping manifestation of climate impacts, it appears that scientists' models have significantly underestimated the speed at which the ice has begun to melt. Paleoclimatologists, who study the history of climates like paleontologists study past life forms, increasingly provide evidence of the instabilities earth's climates can possess. It is virtually certain we have seen just the beginning of future climate surprises.

In another plausible future, global greenhouse gas emissions decline toward zero in the decades ahead, warding off future climate change. Energy-economic models generally offer no way this can happen at a price people seem willing to pay. Greenhouse gas emissions derive from burning fossil fuels like oil and coal, and no country has ever grown rich without burning such fuels. Today, rapidly growing countries like India or China demand all the fossil fuels they can muster to raise living standards for billions of people. Using the best engineering estimates of the performance of future technologies—hydrogen fuels, solar energy, enhanced efficiency, and all the others—the energy-economic models suggest that only strenuous, perhaps unattainable, efforts can reverse the growth of emissions.

Yet history suggests that energy-economic systems are full of surprises that may help solve the climate challenge. Had today's models been run at the beginning of the twentieth century, they would have focused on the problem of growing horse droppings in the urban centers like New York and London, rendered ultimately irrelevant by the automobile, airplane, massive electrification, and the awakening of environmental concern.

The SRES scenarios present a broad spectrum of future emissions paths, ranging from ones that rise fivefold over current levels to ones where emissions drop by the end of the twenty-first century. The key driving forces governing these differing outcomes, organized into four unique storylines, include the rate of economic and population growth, the extent of globalization, and the use of green technology. Measured by their widespread use, the SRES scenarios have been extraordinarily successful. Since their publication in 2000, they have provided the foundation for virtually all serious assessments of future climate change impacts performed by national and state governments and for most studies of the potential costs of reducing emissions.

But measured by their impact on decisionmakers' new understanding of opportunities and dangers, SRES has had far less effect. The scenarios have had little discernable influence over the expectations or mental models that participants bring to debates over the actions needed to slash global emissions of greenhouse gases. Even the arguably most surprising of the scenarios, the "B1" storyline, where rapid global shifts to a service and information economy combine with widespread use of green technology to eventually reduce global emissions, has prompted little discussion about how policymakers might encourage such an outcome. In fact, contrary to the vision of Wack and

Schwartz, SRES's range of quantified emissions paths are ever-present among climate policy studies, while the narrative storylines exist primarily as four short paragraphs perfunctorily quoted if mentioned at all.

The SRES team operated under several constraints common to such large-scale public scenario exercises that virtually preordained such an outcome. The team was prohibited from considering any scenario that included government attempts to reduce greenhouse gas emissions. In part, this dictate flowed from UN politics. UN member states do not agree on climate policies, so SRES could not include them. However, a weakness in the scenario concept itself abetted this constraint—the traditional focus on an external world separate and unaffected by the decisions of the scenarios' users. This may make sense for most private-sector clients, where scenarios might reasonably ignore their ability to affect their consumers' tastes or the overall behavior of the economy. But when the audience is the governments of the United States and other members of the United Nations, there is no external world independent of their choices. Neglecting government policies omits a key potential source of both beneficial and adverse surprise—the ability of purposeful action to catalyze unintended consequences as well as shifts in values, technology, institutions, or some other factor that grows into welcome discontinuous change.

Most important, the SRES team faced a fundamental challenge in choosing which storylines to present. The twenty-first century offers a vast array of plausible futures. Unsuspected and apparently insignificant trends may in the coming decades overturn much currently believed about future emissions and what it takes to control them. The SRES team could run their energy-economic models over dozens of cases, presenting various statistical summaries of the results, but the constraints of traditional scenario analysis required them to tell only three or four stories. Masters like Schwartz and Wack work closely with small groups, gain the trust of their clients, and thus can afford to include a quirky scenario or two that effectively jar the mental models of their small audience. The SRES team, in contrast, addressed the member states of the United Nations and their diverse populations. The team has been subjected to impersonal, extensive, and frequently hostile scrutiny. Their few storylines must stick close to safe, defensible extrapolations of current trends.

Illuminating Key Vulnerabilities of Strategies

In 1953 the United States faced a novel and deeply uncertain national security landscape. With Stalin just dead, nuclear arsenals growing, the Korean War raging, and communists consolidating their rule in Eastern Europe and China, the new U.S. administration of Dwight D. Eisenhower debated whether to continue containment of the Soviet Union or adopt a more aggressive stance. Among the key unknowns was whether time was America's enemy or friend. In an exercise dubbed Project Solarium, Eisenhower organized three teams of advisers and tasked each to make the strongest case for one of three alternative strategies. Team A would champion continued containment, Team B would augment containment with a show of U.S. force, and Team C would replace containment with a rollback of territory held by the Soviet army. The task required the president's advisers to lay out in detail the competing assumptions underlying each strategy about Soviet objectives and American capabilities. In the end, Eisenhower chose continued containment, but the examination of three very different views of the world helped strengthen the intellectual foundation and the legitimacy of the president's choice throughout the government.

Project Solarium was not quite a scenario exercise. But its underlying concept suggests the key to making the scenario concept more broadly useful to today's policymakers. Given the multiplicity of plausible futures, the most important scenarios to consider are those few that most affect the decisionmakers' choice among alternative strategies. A bold and careful strategy should exploit opportunities while avoiding the many ways in which plans can go awry. A small set of scenarios should be carefully chosen to highlight the key trade-offs policymakers face in designing such strategies.

Considering alternative futures that underscore important policy choices is of course not a new concept. The U.S. military has long used "red teams," groups of experts tasked to take the enemy's viewpoint and search for weaknesses in U.S. plans. Any good investor practices due diligence. The Schwartz and Wack scenario school emphasizes finding scenarios that illuminate the strengths and weaknesses of a specific proposed decision.

Yet the combination of novel challenges, decisionmakers' aversion to ambiguity, and the multiplicity of plausible futures make it difficult for such efforts to become a regular input to policy formulation. Traditional scenario analyses like SRES too easily slip into a set of unchallenging futures. Risk analysis of the type that supports regulatory agencies' quantitative cost-benefit analysis relies on estimates of the probability of various events. When faced with novel futures, decisionmakers can too easily choose to believe the most convenient as opposed to the most challenging estimates of potential surprises. Vigorous public debate exposes and corrects policy errors but but often addresses surprise better in hindsight than as an anticipatory device.

New information technology offers an intriguing possibility. It may now be possible to systematize the scenario generation process to the extent that it becomes less an art and more a craft practiced by competent professionals, ultimately like budgeting or accounting. Policymakers can ignore the product of creative and subjective inspiration, but once part of the regular process of policy assessment and formulation, a systematic and reproducible product becomes a much more serious constraint on policymakers' choices.

The key concept here is that of robust adaptive strategies. A robust strategy performs well compared with the alternatives across a very wide range of plausible futures, and an adaptive one evolves over time in response to new information. In practice most policies turn out to be adaptive whether or not they were initially intended that way. In general policymakers also seek strategies that work well no matter what surprises arise. But the human mind can trace only a tiny fraction of the many paths an adaptive strategy can follow into an uncertain future. When confronted with novel challenges, policymakers cannot rely on their experience, intuition, or traditional scenarios to anticipate the paths that stumble across the most relevant surprises.

It has long been possible to use computer simulation models and patterns in data to sketch out millions of plausible futures that explore a vast variety of combinations of events. Until recently, however, such exercises have not been helpful, because no one can usefully examine millions of futures. But today's wealth of interactive computer tools brings new possibilities. Search algorithms analogous to those that help Google users make sense of millions of websites can also delve into vast arrays of computer-generated futures to summarize and characterize their most salient features. Such interactive computer tools can follow the evolution of a potentially robust, adaptive strategy, characterize a small number of key scenarios that represent its most important failures and missed opportunities, and then suggest the best ways to make the strategy more resilient against potential surprise.[7] At the start, there may be many vulnerabilities. But after a few iterations, strategies often become sufficiently robust so that a small number of scenarios succinctly characterize their most important strengths and weaknesses.

This robust decision process importantly encourages policymakers to recast the questions they ask about surprise. The traditional framing for policy analysis requires decisionmakers to first determine the most likely surprises—a perfect recipe for ignoring some surprises and putting too much faith in others. The robust decision approach instead identifies a small number of the most important vulnerabilities to existing plans, inquires about the easiest ways to address them, and only then asks whether these surprises seem sufficiently likely to warrant action. This process can break down many of the psychological and organizational barriers that place the wrong surprises on the agenda in so many policy debates.

This approach has proved successful in a variety of private sector situations as well as in national security and other public policy applications. For instance, a robust decision exercise at RAND explored near-term steps that could help launch the long-term radical changes needed to ensure economic development and environmental quality over the twenty-first century.[8] The exercise tested a near-term strategy with a market-based, cap-and-trade pollution trading system over a huge number of computer-generated futures, each with different combinations of key demographic, economic, environmental, and technology trends. The futures included discontinuous, surprising changes in technology and human values. Participants worked closely with the computer to identify groups of futures—key scenarios—where their initially proposed policy was vulnerable. These scenarios helped sketch a potentially bold and careful approach to sustainable development for the twenty-first century.

Recrafting Scenario Practice for the Twenty-First Century

The United States government significantly improved its management of the economy and business cycle over the course of the twentieth century. The advent of new analytical concepts and methods, such as national income accounting and standard procedures for tracking gross domestic product, provided one important impetus. These tools gave both experts and the lay public a simple quantitative metric they could use to monitor national performance. Once performance could be measured, policymakers could better be held accountable for their economic decisions.

No analogous tools currently exist to effectively hold policymakers faced with a novel future accountable for the choices they do and do not make to exploit surprising opportunities and avoid dangers. Most policymakers will feel pressure to guard against the last surprise, such as hijacking civilian airliners to use as missiles, whether or not it still represents the most important threat. The bold may offer transformational strategies, but find it difficult to engage in serious debate about the risks and how to contain them. The merely careful can emphasize pervasive uncertainty to justify their inaction.

New information technology now offers the possibility of recrafting scenario practice as a means to help policymakers better anticipate the strengths and weaknesses of their approach to surprise and to help others hold them more accountable for their assessments. The robust decision concept could help competent professionals staffing government agencies or nongovernmental organizations reproducibly, rigorously, and systematically identify a small, key set of even highly ambiguous and surprising scenarios and the policy trade-offs they imply. Even in those cases where the full analytic process is not or cannot be carried out, the framing of key scenarios as the avoidable vulnerabilities (including missed opportunities) of robust strategies may begin to change the standards of acceptable due diligence.

Policymakers may not always welcome a critical spotlight on the potential weaknesses of their proposed strategies. But if rigorous assessment of surprise becomes as commonplace as budgeting and accounting, policymakers will find it harder to ignore. Scenarios provide a powerful concept for focusing attention on the unexpected, but to date they have worked best for skilled practitioners working with small groups. Turning scenario practice into a reproducible, operational procedure with the aid of new computer tools may enhance the systematic evaluation of surprise and help nudge America and its leaders toward becoming both bold and careful.

11

Innovation and Adaptation: IT Examples

M. Mitchell Waldrop

Information technology might seem to be the one area where foresight should be almost easy, if only because the trend lines are so obvious. And indeed those trend lines do allow a certain confidence about the general picture. One can be pretty sure, for example, that microprocessors will continue to become exponentially more powerful for at least another decade; that broadband and wireless networks will continue to proliferate; and that electronic devices will become increasingly mobile, increasingly connected, increasingly embedded in buildings, cars, and appliances, and increasingly pervasive in our lives.[1]

What cannot be known with any confidence, however, is how people will actually use this technology. Which trends will dominate? How will the pieces combine? What will it all add up to—if anything?

Judging from computer history itself, moreover, there are at least two reasons why this is so.

Innovations Don't Just Happen

The first reason is that innovations do not just happen—-or at any rate, the truly surprising ones do not. Innovations tend to be the product of individuals who are driven by grand challenges and grand visions—the sort of thing that is almost impossible to see from trend lines alone. Typically, in fact, neither the challenges nor the visions are apparent to anyone who is not already immersed in them.

Back in the 1920s and 1930s, for example, academics tended to be rather contemptuous of raw number crunching, on the theory that a real mathematician or scientist gains insight by abstract reasoning, not reckoning. Slide rules were acceptable, for engineers. But brute number crunching was just arithmetic, a task for desktop adding machines—*women's* work. (The word *computer* was still a job description in the 1920s, and had much the same pink-collar connotation as *typist.*)[2] The building of computing machinery was, by extension, a job for mere tinkerers.

As a result, the road to modern electronic computing began with a handful of very practical pioneers. They were motivated in large part by desperation: modern technology was already beginning to demand calculations on a scale that humans could not manage, even with adding machines. But they were also motivated by a tantalizing glimpse of empowerment: a realization that massive number crunching could open up whole new vistas for engineering, business, and science.

A classic example is Vannevar Bush, who orchestrated the Manhattan Project and all the rest of nation's war-related scientific research during World War II. Bush is probably best known today for his 1945 article about the "memex," a hypothetical knowledge-access tool that could link one concept to the next in a manner that anticipated the World Wide Web by nearly half a century.[3] But he had actually been led to computing starting in the early 1920s, when he was an MIT electrical engineering professor grappling with one of the most vexing technical problems of the day: the instability of electric power networks.[4] The equations that described such a network were straightforward in principle but horrendous in practice, and all but impossible to solve by hand. The result had been a plague of brownouts and blackouts, as power companies struggled to meet soaring demand with high-voltage lines that were designed on the basis of rule-of-thumb and guesswork.

Bush's answer was the Differential Analyzer: an elaborate system of gears and pulleys and parallel rods that took up most of a large room. Completed in 1930, the analyzer was an analog computer, meaning that it represented mathematical variables not by numbers but by measurements—in this case, the rotation of various rods. It was "programmed" by connecting all the rods with gears and pulleys in a way that mimicked the structure of the network equation. In effect, the analyzer became a physical model of the network. From that point, solving the equation was as simple as starting the analyzer's motor. Gears would mesh, pulleys would pull, rods would rotate—and a plotter pen connected to the appropriate rod would neatly trace out the solution on a sheet of graph paper, accurate to 2 percent.

This was a godsend, and not just for the electric power companies. By the mid-1930s, researchers from all over the world were flocking to the analyzer, using it for electrical engineering, atomic physics, seismology, astrophysics, and more. Copies of the machine were under construction or already completed at nearly a dozen sites in the United States and abroad. Bush had secured funding for development of an all-electronic analyzer, and had organized a broad program of analog computing research that would continue at MIT until well after World War II.

The war, of course, created any number of desperate demands for computation, which in turn led to two of the most famous of the pioneering computers: the digital, all-electronic Colossus, which was actually a series of machines created at the British code-breaking center, Bletchley Park, as a tool for cracking the most difficult German ciphers;[5] and the digital, all-electronic ENIAC, which was constructed by engineers at the University of Pennsylvania to calculate artillery trajectories.[6] Starting in mid-1944, moreover, the ENIAC team was joined by the world-renowned, Hungarian-born mathematician John von Neumann, who was also a participant in the super-secret Manhattan Project—and who was looking for computing machines that could help out with the horrendous calculations needed in that effort. Although ENIAC was too late to help in designing the atomic bomb—the machine did not become operational until 1946—von Neumann was inspired nonetheless. After the war, he went on to pioneer what would now be called scientific supercomputing, designing machines and algorithms for weather forecasting and many other types of simulations. And, along with other pioneers such as Alan Turing, he began to pursue a vision of what would now be called artificial intelligence.[7]

Examples such as these suggest that successful technological foresight requires, at a minimum, a careful look at the technological challenges and opportunities facing society as a whole. And forecasters have certainly tried to do that.

But these examples also suggest that it is remarkably difficult to recognize the critical challenges in the abstract, without that personal immersion in the problems. And doing so is even more difficult now that technology has become so thoroughly democratized by microelectronics and the Internet. Back in the early 1970s, to take a famous example, when Intel introduced the first microprocessors, the company assumed that the devices would mostly be used as industrial process controllers. It was the small, but fervent community of electronics hobbyists who started using the chips in "personal minicomputers"—and kicked off the personal computer revolution.[8]

Then in the late 1980s, to take another famous example, the Internet had already begun to spread through academia like the proverbial wildfire—but mainly as a mechanism for e-mail, file sharing, and remote login to mini- and supercomputers. It was Tim Berners-Lee, a physicist and Internet user at the European Center for Particle Physics (CERN), who came up with a way of systematically displaying files in a visual form, and using hyperlinks to jump between them—a system he dubbed the World Wide Web.[9]

And more recently, of course, the web itself has paved the way for eBay, peer-to-peer file sharing, blogging, and a host of other user-driven innovations that no one had anticipated. Today millions, if not billions, of users are coming up with new ideas all around the globe—which makes it effectively impossible for any forecasting methodology to anticipate all of them, much less to know which ones will dominate.

Innovations Don't Happen in Isolation

The second difficulty follows from the first: Even if forecasters could somehow anticipate what the major innovation drivers will be, they would still have a hard time anticipating exactly what form the solution will take. Innovations almost never involve just a single idea, but the convergence of many ideas. And they are not inevitable: they result from societal needs and interactions. The modern digital computer, in particular, required the convergence of at least half a dozen innovations—most involving not just another gadget, but a shift in the way people *thought* about computing. Well into the 1940s, moreover, people were struggling to fit the pieces together in the right way; it took a decade of trial and error (and a war) to get a combination that was workable. Among the most important of these pieces:[10]

—*Digital computing*: solving problems by numerical calculation, as opposed to building a physical model of the problem. It was far from obvious in the beginning that digital was the right way to go, especially given the success of analog machines such as Bush's Differential Analyzer.

—*Binary mathematics:* using 0s and 1s as opposed to the base-10 arithmetic that humans had been using since they first began counting on their fingers.

—*Logic*: recognizing that a simple on-off switch could embody the notions of *true* and *false*, and that a network of such switches could embody all the standard operations of Boolean logic—the operations of binary arithmetic among them. In particular, the network could make comparisons, and thus take alternative courses of action according to circumstances—as in, "If the number X equals the number Y, then do operations P, Q, and R." That ability, in turn, was what made the digital computer so much more than an ultrafast adding machine. A switching circuit could add and subtract—but it could also *decide.*[11] It could work its way through a sequence of such decisions automatically. In a word, it could be programmed.

—*All-electronic switching:* using vacuum tubes for speed, as opposed to mechanical switches. Again, the choice of vacuum tubes was far from obvious in the early days, given that a computer would need tens of thousands of them to do anything useful, and that even a single burnt-out tube could bring the system to a halt. How would the machine ever finish a calculation?

—*Program control:* giving computers the power to carry out long sequences of operations on their own, as opposed to relying on a human operator to press the buttons, watch the meters, load and unload the punch cards, and generally intervene at every step.

—*Stored program control:* storing the program as binary code in the computer's memory, as opposed to reading it in each time from punch cards or paper tape. Once again, the usefulness of this approach was not entirely obvious at the beginning; many of the early computers, including the ENIAC, had at least some of their programming wired into their physical structure. Implementing the stored-program approach was also a good deal harder than it sounds today, given the primitive state of memory technology at the time; no one was able to field a working stored-program computer until the late 1940s. But the stored-program approach had the obvious advantage of convenience: once all the instructions were stored electronically, so that the problem-solving sequence was entirely separate from the hardware, the function of the computer could be changed without having to touch the wiring. Or to put it another way, the act of computation had become an abstraction embodied in what is now known as *software.*

The history of information technology offers many other examples of invention-by-convergence. Among them:

—The modern concept of information and information processing was a synthesis of insights developed in the 1930s and 1940s by Alan Turing, Claude Shannon, Norbert Wiener, Warren McCulloch, Walter Pitts, and John von Neumann.[12]

—The hobbyists who sparked the personal computer revolution in the late 1970s were operating (consciously or not) in the context of ideas that had been around for a decade or more. There was the notion of *interactive* computing, for example, in which a computer would respond to the user's input immediately (as opposed to generating a stack of fanfold printout hours later); this idea dated back to the Whirlwind project, an experiment in real-time computing that began at MIT in the 1940s.[13] There were the twin notions of *individually controlled* computing (having a computer apparently under the control of a single user) and *home* computing (having a computer in your own house); both emerged in the 1960s from MIT's Project MAC, an early experiment in time-sharing.[14] And then there was the notion of a computer as an *open* system, meaning that a user could modify it, add to it, and upgrade it however he or she wanted; that practice was already standard in the minicomputer market, which was pioneered by the Digital Equipment Corporation in the 1960s.[15]

—The Internet as we know it today represents the convergence of (among other ideas) the notion of packet-switched networking from the 1960s;[16] the notion of *inter*networking (as embodied in the TCP/IP protocol), which was developed in the 1970s to allow packets to pass between different networks;[17] and the notion of hypertext—which, of course, goes back to Vannevar Bush's article on the memex in 1945.

Part IV

What Could Be

12

Cassandra versus Pollyanna

A Debate between
James Kurth and Gregg Easterbrook

James Kurth: I am an optimist about the current pessimism, but a pessimist overall. What do I mean by that? Well, I am optimistic about the three particular blindsiding phenomena that have lately received a great deal of attention: catastrophic hurricanes, nuclear terrorism, and the prospect of a global flu pandemic. When it comes to these three phenomena, there is actually little to worry about.

First, turning to the topic of catastrophic hurricanes, or more generally, the phenomena of natural geological catastrophes—hurricanes, floods, tsunamis, volcanoes, or earthquakes—these affect everyone but only in a very limited area. Historically, natural disasters normally take out a city, or maybe a region, but very shortly the society as a whole recovers—even the city itself may, as San Francisco did after the 1906 earthquake and fires, or Tokyo did after the famous Tokyo earthquake of 1923. The Chinese cities devastated by earthquakes in the 1970s recovered rapidly, as well. Of course, if the economic base of the particular city or region is already undermined, the catastrophe may lead to a final decline of that city, as in the Galveston hurricane at the turn of the last century. But other cities then benefit; so, for the most part, natural geological catastrophes have very sharp, narrow, and limited impacts.

Natural biological catastrophes, such as plagues and smallpox and influenza epidemics, influence a large minority, not a majority, population over a wide area. They are thus in a way the inverse of the geological catastrophe. But again, the society normally recovers within a few years, perhaps a generation. Even the notorious 1918 global influenza epidemic that is being discovered again as some earlier prototype of bird flu—left no permanent mark. The histories of the societies affected by it are written almost as if the 1918 epidemic never happened. It was a catastrophe of an order of magnitude equivalent to World War I, and yet it is rarely talked about as a driver of subsequent events. And in general the survivors of these plagues, smallpox, or influenza epidemics tend to be better off than they were before the epidemic.

Now, man-made catastrophes are potentially far more serious, especially wars of mass destruction. Two variations need to be considered. First are the weapons of mass destruction: they are analogous to geological catastrophe. Strategic bombing, as in Japan and Germany during the Second World War, takes out the cities and defeats the society; but, again, society tends to recover within a decade or generation. And that kind of catastrophe—borne by weapons of mass destruction—did have a definitive end and is likely to have a definitive end again. As terrible as it was, it lasted only a year or two, and when it ended, the survivors could begin again.

Second, like the biological catastrophes are what might be called "wars of mass casualties." These are more like biological epidemics in which a large minority are killed over a longer period of time, such as during World War I and World War II. Especially in Britain, France, Germany, and Russia, perhaps one-third or more of the nations' young men died in such wars. (Similar death rates in the American South during the Civil War are the closest thing Americans have ever experienced.) But again, within a decade or generation—if birth rates are reasonably high—the society largely recovers.

Note, however, that neither Britain nor France had fully recovered demographically or psychologically in the twenty years after losing large numbers of their young men in World War I, and that national suffering provided a basis for appeasement in the late 1930s. In contrast, Germany enjoyed a high birth rate during the interwar years. And so the impact of a catastrophe may be deepened by differential demography (a matter to which I will return). But in any event, unlike the natural catastrophes, human or man-made catastrophes have histories that linger on in the collective memory and shape societies as they grow in the future. People care whether they die from human agency or accidents of nature—hence World War I is a causal agent in history, while the flu pandemic, which killed as many people, is not.

So clearly, of these three kinds of catastrophes, the most important from my point of view is the specter of weapons of mass destruction; and those could be either nuclear weapons or biological weapons. That is very serious, indeed; but considering everything said up to now, there may be grounds for optimism that even if a catastrophe should happen—if terrorists should inflict two or three nuclear attacks upon the United States, or perhaps even a biological attack—perhaps as the models of previous weapons of mass destruction and previous epidemics suggest, American society would be able to recover fairly soon.

But notice some differences. What is relatively new for modern American society is the specter of a barbarian enemy who is willing and even wishes to destroy the entire society, indeed all of modern Western society. Islamist terrorists are literally genocidal in their attitudes toward the West. Another difference is that the terrorist cells thrive within the very societies they wish to harm. The task of stopping them is harder than definitively defeating a nation-state, like Germany and Japan, or containing one for a long time, like the Soviet Union or Communist China. Instead, the West faces a network of persons motivated by an intense hatred who will attack repeatedly until Western society is destroyed.

To find an historical analogy for this challenge, one must go back to pre-modern, perhaps even pre-Western, eras of barbarians such as the Goths who overran Rome, or the notorious Huns and the Mongols in the Middle East or in Russia. Modern Western societies have never faced barbarians who wish to destroy them utterly and potentially have the technological capacity to do so. Even the Nazis and the Communists preserved something of a modern society when they conquered a place. Successful attacks by a barbarian enemy would be different.

Historically, these barbarian societies, even those with technological equality, were for the most part, in the end, defeated. After all, there was a time when Europeans in America were confronted with what they considered to be a barbarian society that had acquired weapons and technology from the pioneers, and these Indian societies were ultimately defeated. But what is crucial to the outcome of such struggles is that the civilized societies are growing faster or are more vital economically, and *especially* demographically, than the barbarian ones. The cases of Rome versus the Goths and the Huns versus the Mongols were cases where the civilized societies were in demographic decay or decline. So it is extremely important to look at the demography; indeed, I would say: *demography is destiny.*

A couple of generations ago, Fritz Stern, a famous historian of Germany, wrote a book reporting that the German minorities, or even majorities, in many parts of eastern Europe felt their culture was being overshadowed by the rising culture of the Slavic peoples around them.[1] Such feelings were ultimately based on the politics of demographic despair, of differential birth rates.

We now have in the West societies that, for the first time in Western history in the last two or three generations, are suffering demographic declines rather than demographic increases. Remember what happened when France and Britain suffered demographic decline after World War I: their robustness and resiliency after the bloodletting of World War I was very weak, where conversely, Germany and Russia, which experienced demographic increase, were able to get their act together all too effectively in the years thereafter.

So today three factors are in conjunction—weapons of mass destruction, a barbarian enemy, and demographic decline—that is utterly new to the West, and, indeed, new to the modern age generally. Now, if weapons of mass destruction alone were the threat, the West could easily survive or thrive. After all, that was the condition the United States faced when it dealt with the Soviet Union and China in the midst of the cold war. Or, facing weapons of mass destruction and Islamic terrorism only, the West could fight and probably win a relentless, ruthless war against Islamist terrorists. But with the conjunction of weapons of mass destruction, the genocidal intent of Islamist forces, and its own demographic decay, the West cannot engage in a long war where it both inflicts and has inflicted upon it the prospect and reality of millions of casualties. The United States has never experienced millions of casualties, nothing like what Britain, France, Germany, and Russia experienced in World Wars I and II. The closest analogy to this, once again, is the experience of the South in the Civil War, and that certainly changed Southern culture and the path of Southern history tremendously.

Today the West is confronted with the reality of demographic decay—that is to say, so-called net reproduction rates of roughly 1.3 children per couple—in contrast to demographic vitality in majority Islamic countries in the world and among the Islamic minorities in Europe. This differential demography is having a big impact that will create new and widening cultural and demographic disparities.

Now, the sources of the demographic decay in the West can be easily specified. First, the postindustrial, or "information-age," economy has not only brought prosperity but also made children unnecessary to the economy, be it agrarian or industrial. The West simply does not need a lot of brawny young laborers.

Second, the modern welfare state has also made children unnecessary because, at least until recently, people thought the state would provide for their old age, not their children, which was the historical pattern.

Third, women in the postindustrial society and the welfare state are entering into full occupational equality, even occupational identity with men. To such women, children are not only unnecessary but a burden.

These particular socioeconomic phenomena also generate particular ideologies: consumerism, the welfare phenomenon, the ideology of social democracy, and feminism. These come together in the ideology of expressive individualism. And why should expressive individualists want to be burdened with many children? Indeed, the norm is one child, giving rise to reproduction rates in the European and European-descended populations of 1.3 or 1.4 children per couple. It is the very economic, social, and political achievements and characteristics of the modern West that have given rise to this phenomenon.

The achievements of the West are all about economic prosperity, social security, gender equality, liberal democracy, and philosophic individualism. This is what the modern West is all about, and exactly this is what we are hoping to spread to the rest of the globe. But these very achievements make the globalist society and the Western image vulnerable to demographic decay and to a substantial protracted war against Islamic terrorist networks armed with weapons of mass destruction, demographic vitality, and an alternative vision of a global civilization—that is to say the global *umma* of Islam.

Gregg Easterbrook: It is a great honor to stand here under the banner of the new *American Interest* magazine, but I should warn all of you that, having listened to Cassandra Kurth talk about demography, I'm planning on starting a magazine called the *Prurient Interest.* I hadn't thought about demography quite in those terms before. In my defense let me say that my wife and I have three children, so we are doing our part; and I can assure you my wife is indeed an expressive individualist, nonetheless.

I am Pollyanna tonight, a role I accepted knowing full well the challenges that attend it. Pollyannaism has a bad name: the word *Pollyanna* has come to mean someone who is oblivious to the bad events occurring around him or her. This is a misuse of the term; it is Doctor Pangloss, Voltaire's idiot, who is like that. Pollyanna, in contrast, was a great literary character, and I have here some pictures of her. Here is Hayley Mills in the 1960–61 movie. In literature, Pollyanna had great accomplishments—she went to the town of Beldingsville, where everyone was miserable and unfriendly, and people scurried into their houses and refused to be neighborly with each other. And by being relentlessly optimistic, she reformed the entire town of Beldingsville all by herself. Now compare this with Cassandra: Cassandra gave her warnings, but Troy was destroyed anyway, and she ended up being sold into slavery. What, then, did Cassandra accomplish? Not a good résumé, no.

What do these two tales show? That there is a structural difference between optimism and pessimism. An optimist is not someone who is unaware of the many problems of the world, but one who believes that problems can be overcome. A pessimist believes not that there are necessarily more problems, or worse ones, but rather that the problems will overcome us instead of the other way around. This is the main structural difference between the two.

I want to argue that nearly all objective trends in the world are today positive and have been so especially since the end of the cold war. This is an especially positive moment in history, an almost glowing one by my estimation, and the fact that so many speak so negatively and pessimistically about it is really quite puzzling. Of course, low-probability catastrophes are possible, but by definition unlikely. Moreover, events that rarely occur but were relatively likely in the past will probably remain rare and be relatively unlikely in the future. Some low-probability catastrophes do worry me, but the optimistic list is more interesting and relevant to our future.

Why is this? It is due to what can be called the liberation of freedom. In May of 1940 the world was genuinely on the brink of catastrophe. Since then, things have been mainly positive because the defeat of tyranny by liberty has set us globally on the right course. And the lesson that comes of May 1940 forward is not only that liberty is better than tyranny—that has always been known—but also that liberty is *stronger* than tyranny. This is a very important lesson. When historians look back at the twentieth century, one of the things that will pop out at them is that virtually every time liberty and tyranny met on the field of battle, liberty prevailed. That makes me most optimistic about the future.

Democracy is now advancing throughout the world. In 1975 one-third of the world's nations held true multiparty elections; today two-thirds do. That is a spectacular improvement in a short period of time. Many new democracies are very fitful, of course; many things could go wrong and some probably will. But the fact that the former Soviet Union, most of Latin America, almost all of the old Eastern bloc, and even China are moving one way or another toward democracy is tremendously positive. In all the world the only large bloc resisting liberty is the Arab world, and sooner or later it is going to dawn on Arab societies that this is the reason why they are weak, and then they will change.

Second, the cold war ended without a shot being fired. Not only is that a spectacular development in and of itself but equally important is the resulting decline in the number of nuclear bombs. At the peak of the cold war, there were 50,000 strategic warheads in the world, enough to literally end all life on this planet. Today more than half of them have been decommissioned; some are being physically disassembled; all the big city-buster bombs, the bombs of more than one megaton, have already been disassembled; and current treaties will drive the Russian Federation and the United States down to less than 5,000 total strategic warheads—still a big number, but 90 percent of the doomsday arsenal will be gone. That is an incredibly positive development, but most people simply take it for granted these days, and readily find other things to complain and worry about.

Then there is the sharp decline of war. For the last fifteen years, the Iraq war not withstanding, studies all show that the intensity of combat—defined by the number of wars in the world, the number of combat casualties, and the number of subsidiary casualties (people who die as refugees)—has been in steady decline. Today a person's chance of dying by violence, crime, or warfare is the lowest it has ever been in human history. In the year 2000 some sort of milestone was passed when more people died in traffic accidents globally than in combat. Not that dying in a car crash is anything to celebrate, but this is nevertheless a fortunate indicator for our future, and those numbers continue to move in opposite directions. Graphs of combat deaths—that is, deaths of soldiers in combat and deaths of civilians associated with combat—keep going down and traffic deaths keep going up. So obviously something needs to be done about traffic, especially in developing countries, but it is a kind of luxury to worry more about traffic than about combat.

As warfare declines, military spending is declining—another trend that is often ignored. Stated in current dollars, annual global military spending peaked in 1985 at $1.3 trillion; it has fallen every year since, to the current $1 trillion. The global population rose by one-fifth in that period, meaning that *per capita* military spending went down a lot; in 1985 the world spent $260 (in current dollars) per person, per year on military arms; last year it spent $167. That is a decline of almost one-third, adjusted for inflation. Is the decline in war being caused by the decline in military spending? Or is the decline in military spending a result of the decline of war? No matter, really, for our purposes here: both are good.

And there is still more good news. Predicted Malthusian catastrophes have not happened. The literature of the 1960s—not just that of Paul Ehrlich, but of many others as well—widely predicted that half of India would have starved to death by now, that more than a billion people would have starved to death globally, that a Hobbesian war of all against all would prevail in most developing nations, leading to total breakdown of societies. Instead, in some recent years India has been a net exporter of grain, and malnutrition has fallen steadily throughout the world. About 17 percent of the developing world today is malnourished; that is a shockingly high figure, but it is also the lowest such figure in recorded human history. Again, even as the global population has more than doubled in the postwar era, malnutrition has steadily declined.

Plague catastrophes have not occurred, either. AIDS is awful but it is reasonably contained; Ebola, SARS (severe acute respiratory syndrome), and West Nile virus, the three most recent outbreak diseases, have killed far fewer people than lightning. Avian flu, which we have heard so much about, had killed 186 people as of May 24, 2007. The 1918 pandemic, remember, occurred in a time of extremely poor public health, and just after a half-global war where many nations had experienced brutal combat for five years. Public health and sanitary conditions were poor. The two later flu pandemics, in 1957 and 1968, occurred when public health care was much better, and death ratios were far lower as a result. If any kind of transmissible avian flu develops in 2006 or 2007, it is going to occur in a world that is mainly at peace, where public health is better still, and where the likelihood of some runaway effect is very small—though, of course, it cannot be ruled out altogether.

There is a viral pandemic occurring in the world right now: the Rhoda virus pandemic, which has killed 1.5 million people since avian flu was detected three years ago. There is a reliable vaccine that prevents it, but not much is being done to deal with the Rhoda virus because it affects only the developing world; whereas the United States is spending a huge amount of money to guard its borders against mutant chickens. Runaway genetic effects are not observed in nature, but they cannot be ruled them out. So we have the popularity of movies like *Outbreak*, with Dustin Hoffman; or the ridiculous novel, *The Cobra Event*, which Bill Clinton sat reading in the White House (the plot involves one single particle of weaponized smallpox that kills everyone in New York City within twenty-four hours); or ABC's bird flu disaster movie in which one single person exposed to bird flu in Asia infects most of the United States—and all of American society is in ruins in about a week. It would be nice if most people knew enough to distinguish what might be called sci-hysteria-fiction from real science, but they mainly don't. Now that *is* sad.

It is also worth noting that attempts to use biological or chemical weapons in warfare have generally been unsuccessful. The history of the use of chemical weapons, including in World War I, is that they are less destructive pound for pound than explosives. Weaponized smallpox was accidentally released in the Soviet Union in 1979, where it killed sixty-eight people. That is sixty-eight individual tragedies, but nothing like what exists in the popular imagination.

On to a nicer subject—the global economy is booming. Global growth has been above 5 percent a year for many years in a row, and global growth is greater than population growth, which is the key: as long as global economic growth remains ahead of global population growth, things will look positive. China and India are booming at around 8 percent a year, and most currencies are stable. Hyperinflation is currently rare, although it could come back. Globalization was sold as something that would make all the countries of the world better off, not just the wealthy ones, and so far that has been the experience. Benjamin Friedman, the former head of the economics department at Harvard, argues that historically the world becomes more liberal and democratic during times of economic growth, while stagnation is associated with repression and unhappy societies.[2] The conclusion is that society should root for economic growth because liberal democracy will accompany it.

Most important of all, the biggest economic gains are in the developing nations, not in the West. More progress has been made against poverty in the past fifty years than in the previous five thousand. Rates of extreme poverty in the developing world are still a huge problem, but they are in steep decline. The developing world's extreme poverty rate was 30 percent in 1990; it is 21 percent today; and if current trends continue, it will fall to just 10 percent by 2015. Global per capita income has doubled in real dollars since 1975, and even if the income of Western and Arab petroleum states is subtracted from that figure, global per capita real income has still increased almost 60 percent. In 1975, 1.6 billion people in the developing world lived at the standard the United Nations calls "medium development"—roughly, the living conditions of a village in Portugal. Today, 3.6 billion people live in medium development; in thirty years two billion people have moved up and out of abject poverty to middle development—a spectacular achievement by any reasonable measure.

Another positive factor is global equality. In 1950 the developing world produced 29 percent of the world's income; today it produces 44 percent of the world's income. If current trends continue, the developing world will pass the Western world as a generator of the world's income within two generations.

Literacy rates are rising; education rates are rising, especially for girls—and that is very important. Access to information through the Internet and other inexpensive means of communication is expanding, and knowledge is like toothpaste: it cannot be put back into the tube. The apparatchiks of the former Soviet Union spent three decades using brutal means to attempt to put knowledge of the West back into the tube, and they eventually gave up. They concluded not that they were not being brutal enough, but that it is simply impossible to withdraw knowledge from society.

Resources make for optimism, too. No primary resource in the world is in short supply or is likely to become so, including oil. The only resource specialists worry about right now is fresh water in China and the Middle East; everything else seems fairly plentiful. This is important because global production must increase. In his book Ben Friedman estimates that if the goal is to raise the standard of the entire world by 2050 to a state of medium development, taking into account projected population increases during that time, global economic output must quadruple. That will make for a lot of resource consumption. Fortunately, all forms of pollution except for greenhouse gases are in decline, at least in the Western countries. Of course, greenhouse gases are a big exception. But in the Western countries, which have clean technologies and strong antipollution regulations, all forms are in decline. In the last thirty years acid rain in the United States has decreased by 60 percent. Even though Americans burn twice as much coal as they used to, smog has decreased by 40 percent. Even though there are now twice as many automobiles that are driven three times as many miles, water pollution is down by 90 percent. All of these things have happened in a period of strong economic growth. The same trends have not yet reached the developing world, but they can, if the developing world adopts the same kind of clean technology and imposes strong regulations and sticks to them.

Pollution is down because nearly all technological trends are currently benign. All trends in manufacturing reveal factories using fewer resources and less energy and generating less waste. For example, General Electric builds new diesel engines that, at 800 tons, use less than half as much fuel and produce about 70 percent less diesel emissions as did previous models. They are expected to last for one hundred years. And this trend is found throughout technology: most products use fewer resources and less energy than the products they replace, and they are less dangerous to consumers as safety standards keep rising.

This is true in military affairs, as well; nuclear weapons aside, many conventional weapons are becoming steadily less dangerous as they are made more accurate. During the first Gulf War in 1991, the standard bomb the United States dropped on Iraq weighed 2,000 pounds; in 2003 the standard bomb dropped on Iraq weighed 500 pounds but was much more accurate. The U.S. Air Force is developing a new bomb that weighs 250 pounds and is pinpoint accurate, and future models are expected to weigh 100 pounds or less.

Not every trend in technology is benign, but most of them are. People are living longer: the population explosion of the twentieth century was not caused by more births but by fewer deaths. At the beginning of the twentieth century, global life expectancy was thirty-seven years; at the beginning of the twenty-first century, it was sixty-six years, and that includes places like Afghanistan,

Pakistan, Congo, and other troubled parts of the world. I am optimistic that these positive trends will continue. At the same time, trends in popular music are really bad, and I just do not see anything that will change that. That is a problem.

James Kurth: At some level I agree with everything that Gregg said—in the sense that I certainly agree with all the facts and the essential phenomena he described. I also think that in the spring of 1914, we would have discovered similar facts and phenomena: economically, politically, culturally, educationally, everything was getting better in every way in most places. And yet something went wrong. It is true that if the trend lines as they were in the spring of 1914 are projected forward, things continue to get better up to the present day. But there were those big dips that started in August of 1914 and then reappeared in September 1939, and so on. Trend lines and broad quantitative statistics are important phenomena, yes; but they can be completely disrupted by tiny qualitative changes.

In addition to questioning the significance of positive trend lines, let me now make a much more ancient distinction between what might be called the mechanistic metaphor and the organic metaphor. If one tends to think of societies as a kind of mechanistic ensemble, bits and pieces of which can be added or subtracted discretely, then one can imagine an optimistic and quantitative step-by-step improvement. But if one thinks organically, one can see that a slight change in the body politic or the body social can make a tremendous difference. It might be true, for example, that one's body is getting better and better all the time. But if only a small part of the body, the eyes, for example, or a strategically placed heart valve, should go bad, the entire body will suffer a catastrophe. I tend to think in terms of the organic conception, and so I can agree with everything Gregg says quantitatively but disagree with the qualitative implications.

Gregg Easterbrook: Let me start my response by saying that I do not think about demographics in quite the same way you do, Jim. It probably is inevitable that because of demographic vigor the United States will at some point not be the world's dominant power as it is today. Is that necessarily bad? I don't know. The United States will still be important. If England in 1950—when the British Empire had just crumbled, and there was a great sense of gloom among the English that they would no longer control the world—is compared with the England of today, 2006 is the best time ever to be a citizen of the United Kingdom. The place is wonderful, pollution is way down, public housing is finally acceptable, the theater scene is the most vibrant it has ever been. I would even go as far as to say that the food is good. So if there is a future in which Western nations are less powerful than they are today because of demographics, as long as their people are still free and can raise their children the way they want, I don't think that would bother me so much.

But now it is time, I think, to tell you what low-probability events *do* worry me. One is actually a high-probability event—global warming. The scientific evidence is now pretty persuasive. I was skeptical as recently as ten years ago; I am no longer skeptical. We have to do something about it. It is not going to be *The Day after Tomorrow,* where the world ends overnight, but the likelihood is that climate change will not be to our liking, especially as it affects agriculture. The world is very balanced in agricultural production right now. It is critical that agricultural yields always exceed population growth, and if there is some kind of climate change, that could stop being the case. But I am still an optimist in the sense that global warming is not going to be the insolvable problem some people think. Global warming is basically an air pollution problem. All previous air pollution problems have been solved more rapidly and at much lower costs than most observers projected. Urban smog, chlorofluorocarbons, acid rain—they have all been much cheaper to fix than lots of people anticipated. Global warming looks daunting now because no one has really tried to fix it. It will take a while to fix, but it will not, I am sure, cost anything near the amount some think.

Comet, asteroid, and large meteor strikes worry me, too. Obviously, they are improbable in anybody's lifetime, but the world has been hit by big things in the past, and it will be hit by big things again in the future. And even though it is improbable in one person's lifetime, there is no guarantee that some big ball of ice or rock is not hurtling toward Trenton, New Jersey, right now. And I say that partly in jest because, after all . . . Trenton?! But an asteroid strike, as Judge Posner has written, could be more deadly than all the tragedies of history combined. And it does drive me slightly crazy that NASA spends $10 billion a year on the space station project, on this floating Motel 6, where the guys do nothing but drink Tang and take each other's blood pressure. There is just no purpose to this space station other than to spend money and make NASA into a paracelebrity agency so that it can get still more money. That $10 billion could be used to do a very rigorous study on near-earth objects and try to come up with some way to deflect one if it is coming at us. If the National Aeronautics and Space Administration succeeded in deflecting an asteroid heading toward the Earth—that would be, oh, let's just say, the single most important achievement in human history. So it would be nice if that issue was being addressed.

There is another natural calamity that arrests my attention: a nearby supernova explosion, which would probably end life on earth. Many scientists now think that past periods of mass extinction were in sync with nearby (in cosmic terms) supernova explosions. There is nothing we can do about that, except, maybe, some very persuasive praying.

And the final thing that my expressive individualist wife and I worry about, raising three kids in the Washington area, is a crude atomic warhead going off in Washington or New York. I think there is a chance that will happen in my lifetime, and with each passing year, my worry about it increases. That is because the amount of nuclear materials in the world, the amount of technology in the world, increases. Of all the things that depress me, when I let myself think about them, that is what depresses me the most, not only because such an event would be a human tragedy, but because the United States, if not the entire world, would be plunged into a long and deep economic depression. In a week after an atomic bomb went off on American soil, a hundred million people would die around the world as the United States military nuked every military facility in every nation that could in any way have had anything to do with it. I think an age of darkness would follow such an event. So if I had a pessimist's money to spend, that is what I would be spending it on. Except I am an optimist, so guess what? I'm keeping my money.

James Kurth: If I may, please, a brief rejoinder about demography. There was, a long time ago, a Roman slogan about the family that went like this: "sanctity, fidelity, progeny." The ideal family came together under these three dimensions. Sanctity—that the family would be sanctified by the religion of the day, originally the Roman religion, then later the Christian religion. Fidelity—yes, fidelity—in other words, married for life. Progeny was the third necessary condition. Sanctity, fidelity, and progeny. The early fathers of the Christian church were very conscious of the population decline in pagan Rome. And they reinvented and reinvigorated this Roman model into a Roman Christian model. And that increased the population of Christians, while the population of pagans was declining.

Now, sociologists have looked into this and determined that religious conviction tended to correlate with higher birthrates. And so it remains: the "red" states have higher birthrates than the "blue" states. Conservatives may outproduce liberals within America, even if they do not outthink them. But more seriously, from the point of view I am talking about, there has been a kind of latter day, second-rate alpine glow of religious identity, which was patriotic identity, in America over the past several decades. So the sociologists would say it is the conjunction of the religious identity and the patriotic identity in Americans, along with, of course, robust rates of immigration, that produces demographic vitality. It is no surprise that demographic rates are lower in Europe than any other place on the planet, with the exception of course of Japan, which is also postnational and postreligious.

13

Global Discontinuities

A Discussion with
Owen Harries, Itamar Rabinovich, Niall Ferguson, and Scott Barrett

Owen Harries: The two terms *Australia* and *surprises* do not often appear in the same sentence. Australia is generally thought of as predictable, stable, dependable, but not surprising. It is worth remembering, however, that the areas adjacent to Australia have experienced their shares of surprises. Two examples: In 1940 the Southwest Pacific was one of the most inconsequential backwaters in the world, an area in which nothing of importance ever happened, which contained nothing of any strategic interest. Only two years later, locations such as Guadalcanal and the Coral Sea were the scenes of decisive events in world politics, and Japanese submarines were in Sydney Harbor. A quarter century later, in the mid-1960s, postcolonial Southeast Asia was probably the most unstable, violent, and unpromising area in the world. Arthur Schlesinger, Jr., fresh from his stint in the Kennedy administration, described the region pretty accurately as "an underdeveloped sub-continent, filled with fictitious states, in vague chaotic and unpredictable revolutionary ferment."[1] The new city-state of Singapore was widely though to be unviable. It did not even have its own drinking water. Local cultures and religions of the area were plausibly said to be incompatible with capitalism—all this on the eve of what turned out to be one of the most rapid transformations in modern history, when, within a decade and a half, Southeast Asia provided the definitive model for successful emergence from third world backwardness. It even developed a regional organization, ASEAN, or the Association of Southeast Asian Nations, which was successful in maintaining peaceful and harmonious relations between states.

So the area is capable of producing surprises. As to possible surprises in the near future, I offer a couple of suggestions. The past forty years of Southeast Asia's history will turn out to have been a transient golden age between times of trouble rather than a period representing the foundation of a durable stability and prosperity. Why? Not because of economic problems and dangers such as those of 1997–98. The precipitating event, or one of them, may well be the disintegration of Indonesia, the largest and most powerful state in the region. It is a country with serious internal stresses. It lost East Timor a few years ago in rather humiliating circumstances. It has subsequently been forced to cede substantial autonomy to Aceh in northern Sumatra after years of unsuccessful attempts to crush a resistance movement there. It faces a serious independence movement in resource-rich Melanesian West Papua. There is running violence between Muslims and Christians in various parts of the country. And Jamaah al-Islamiya, a serious, active, homegrown Islamist terrorist organization, has perpetrated a series of violent acts.

In addition, Indonesia is in the process of making a serious effort to become democratic. However desirable this is in the short run, it involves the danger of a comparatively weak and unstable leadership in a country that is accustomed to being led by strong men. Disintegration could well be the outcome of all this. A second possible outcome could be the emergence of Indonesia as an Islamist state, based on an alliance between the armed forces and extreme Islamic elements. Islam in Indonesia is usually discussed in terms of moderation. But it is worth remembering that there was from independence through the mid-1960s an extreme element, represented by Darul Islam. Although the Islamist element in Indonesia is currently small, it is also worth remembering that small but determined minorities can achieve great success in unstable conditions—the Bolshevik Party in Russia had a membership of only 23,000 at the beginning of 1917.

Either of these outcomes would be enormously destabilizing, both to the immediate region and more widely. If one were to superimpose Indonesia on a map of Europe, it would reach from Ireland to Turkey. There are some 13,000 islands. Vital trade routes move through the region. Most of the oil that goes to China and Japan moves through the region, so any disintegration or instability in this area would be a vital concern to both of those countries. Terrorism almost certainly would increase, and the prospect of mass migration would be a serious one for Australians to worry about.

Another less spectacular but not unimportant surprise may be in the offing: a serious change in the character of the U.S.-Australian alliance. For fifty years the alliance has been marked by undeviating devotion on Australia's part, a willingness to march in lockstep with its great ally. "All the way with LBJ," "we'll go a-waltzing Matilda with you," and more recently what has been happening with respect to Iraq. There is a good chance that this mode of behavior will change, that Australia's alliance conduct will alter significantly, becoming much more qualified, discriminating, and selective. That change will result in part from the Iraqi experience, which has produced an increased awareness of American fallibility and shortcomings. But two other fundamental reasons lie behind this impending change, one of the push kind and one of the pull kind.

The push will come from the increasing incompatibility between the outlooks and interests of the two countries. The United States is determined to change the world profoundly, so that it conforms with American notions of how the world should be. Australia is essentially satisfied with the way the world is, with its disproportionate share of the good things of the world, and it is therefore apprehensive that any great change may leave it worse off. In other words, the push will come from the increasing tension between the interests of a revisionist superpower and those of a status quo middle power.

As for the pull, that will come from Australia's increasingly strong relationship with China. Currently that relationship is based mainly, though not entirely, on the compatibility of the two economies: China's insatiable appetite for minerals and energy, and Australia's enormous capacity to satisfy it. Trade between the two countries has been increasing at well over 20 percent a year, and China has already displaced the United States as Australia's second biggest trading partner; if things go on this way, China will displace Japan before very long, as well. But it is not just a matter of economics. China in recent years has been very successful in extending its influence in Southeast Asia as a moderate, reasonable actor, not throwing its weight around. Fear of the downward thrust of Communist China, which was for many years the unspoken assumption that underlay the alliance, especially from Australia's side, has rapidly diminished.

Australia's behavior with respect to the alliance will therefore become much more discriminating, qualified, and selective. This might not worry some people; it will very much worry those who believe in the theory of Anglophone compatibility throughout the world.

Itamar Rabinovich: In the British Foreign Service, the method has long been that every quarter, the embassy sends home a report that ends with a predictive paragraph. So it was that in January 1954, the British ambassador in Damascus sent home the last quarterly report for 1953. Syria was then ruled by a military dictator named Adib al-Shishakli, and the ambassador was very sanguine about Shishakli, and so the predictive paragraph thus ended with the sentence that unless he committed suicide, Shishakli was here to stay. In February 1954 Shishakli was deposed, and Whitehall held its breath for the ambassador's first dispatch. When it arrived, it became an instant classic because it opened with the following sentence: "A close scrutiny of the events that have unfolded in Damascus in the recent days would inevitably lead one to the conclusion that Shishakli committed political suicide."[2]

This is one way of saying that one does expect surprises and discontinuities in the Middle East, an area that in the last several decades has been the scene of warfare, coups, and other unexpected developments. In 1967 war broke out unexpectedly for Israel. The October 1973 war was a strategic intelligence surprise. The quadrupling of oil prices after that war was a surprise for the world. The Iraqi capture of Kuwait in August 1990, developments in Iraq, developments in Lebanon—there is a long list of events that surprised either actors in the region or international global actors.

Yet there is a pattern. Look at the region as it was around 1970, and look at it now. What were the decisive elements in 1970? The Middle East was a battlefield for the cold war and Soviet-American competition. In the Arab world the dominant force was Arab nationalism and the quest for Arab unity. The Arab-Israeli conflict seemed to defy resolution. The two former imperial powers that had dominated the region in earlier centuries, Turkey and Iran, were out of the game in the Middle East, with Turkey looking to Europe and Iran focusing on its immediate area in the Persian Gulf. A series of regimes that came into power around 1970 developed reliable techniques for staying in power. The regimes in Egypt, Libya, Syria, Saudi Arabia, and the Gulf that were in or came to power at that time are still in power today. So there has been a surprising degree of regime stability since 1970, with Lebanon and Iraq being, of course, the two exceptions.

Look at the region now. There is no cold war; there is one paramount superpower. Arab nationalism has been replaced by political Islam as a dominant force. The Arab-Israeli conflict has been replaced by an Arab-Israeli peace process, intermittent, not always successful, but it has replaced the state-to-state conflict. Turkey still looks to Europe, but it is now more Islamic and more active in the region. And Iran, of course, has become a major player in the politics of the region. Most of the regimes are still in place, and, of course, there have been several wars in the region, most recently in Iraq and southern Lebanon. What can be expected next by way of unsurprising surprises? Where will new surprise come from?

I would look at major regime change in one of several countries. Several are candidates not for a coup, nor even for a regime change, but for a far-reaching revolution that would have an impact similar to what happened in Lebanon or Iraq. Think of what even a regime change, let alone a revolution, in Saudi Arabia would mean for the region or the world. Several countries are ripe for regime change. In certain countries regime change could even lead to an undoing of the area—and of the order that was established in the aftermath of World War I. Iraq may soon be practically divided into three states. This could be the first crack in the wall of the 1921 settlement, and it could have far-reaching consequences in that regard. Of course, there could also be a new war, either a regional war or an external intervention into the region, and both could happen simultaneously or nearly so. An internal collapse might also provoke war, as the collapse of Lebanon led to the Israeli invasion of Lebanon in 1982. It would be safe to assume that one or more of these unsurprising surprises—or expected discontinuities—will take place in the Middle East in the coming years. The region will continue to provide the world with its share of instability. It will continue to be the global equivalent of a bad neighborhood.

Niall Ferguson: We tend to assume that low-probability, high-impact events—I'm going to call them *lippies* (LPHIs)—are important. But in reality, if there is a way of attaching probability to a LPHI, it has probably already been priced in. So in that sense, LPHIs are not very interesting. Much more interesting, it may be argued, are high-probability, high-impact events, which I shall call *hippies* (HPHIs). Rather surprisingly, human beings—whether they are ordinary human beings or members of the elite commentariat—quite often ignore these.

What should human beings worry about? The first thing is heart disease, which is the principal cause of avoidable mortality worldwide—around 16 million deaths every year, according to the World Health Organization. Someone in my age group is six times more likely to die of heart disease than of war-related causes. Or, taking the world as a whole, a given forty-year-old is seven times more likely to die of AIDS than of non-war-related violence.

Another thing ordinary human beings should worry about is road traffic. Americans have a one in seventy-seven chance in the course of their lives of being killed in road accidents, and that is a far more likely cause of death than terrorism. In my own country, the United Kingdom, around 3 percent of deaths are estimated to result from external causes of mortality. Of these, 18 percent are caused by transportation accidents, 20 percent are caused by what is politely called self-harm, only 2 percent are caused by assault, and in the last year for which I have statistics, only 2 out of all 536,000 deaths were the result of war.

So heart disease and car crashes are the two things we should worry about. When people are asked in opinion polls, "What is the most important issue facing the country today?" British people ought to say, first, our lousy driving; second, our lousy diet; and third, our recurrent bouts of depression, because those three things are the major causes of avoidable death in Britain. What they actually say is only partly rational. For example, worry at the moment is centered on the National Health Service. Now that has a certain rationality. If someone expects to fall victim either to a road accident or to a heart attack, it is probably rational to want the government to put on a better health service than Britain currently has to offer. But it does seem to me slightly odd to take that view; it would be much better, surely, to prevent these mishaps in the first place.

The other two concerns that loom large in British opinion polls—and here there is a strong similarity with the United States—are immigration and race relations, and foreign affairs and international terrorism. But of course everyone knows that the likelihood of falling victim to an attack by an immigrant, or the descendant of an immigrant, is much lower than the likelihood of being run over or killed in a collision by a native-born bad driver. People know that the long-term trend in terrorism in the recent past has been a decline in the number of international attacks from a peak in the mid-1980s. Over that long-term period, many more terrorist incidents have happened in Latin America than in Britain or the United States. September 11, 2001, was and remains an outlier. So it seems to me that a fundamental problem must be recognized: People prioritize the wrong risks. They tend to attach significance to exciting and perhaps newsworthy risks, rather than to prosaic, or, I hesitate to say it, pedestrian risks.

There is a similar myopia among intellectuals, scholars, and policy analysts. Whether members of this group are engaged in the more lucrative pursuit of forecasting for financial gain, or whether they do it just for fun or for the middling remuneration of the think-tank world, when they try to assess what we should be worried about, or what politicians should be worried about, they tend to identify the wrong things. If I were to make a list, or take a poll, of the favorite low-probability, high-impact events of the people in this room, the following five sources of possible LPHIs are likely to be identified: Iran's nuclear weapons program, Iraq's descent into civil war, Gazprom's power to blackmail European gas importers, the hurricane season in the Gulf of Mexico, and of course the biggest source of a LPHI of all, Ben Bernanke's mouth. But these are all priced in, and in that sense, they are not terribly interesting, even though they are events to try to avoid or to prepare for.

What LPHIs and HPHIs are not priced in? Well, another September 11 is not priced in because of the difficulty of attaching probability to it. An avian flu pandemic is not priced in. A computer virus that would shut down Google has not been priced in, although that would have a really quite an extraordinary effect. The potential for hostilities between the United States and China over Taiwan is not priced in. But none of those are particularly interesting, either, because the probability of their happening is quite low.

One possibility, though, is really interesting, because it resembles the likelihood of being killed in a car crash or of having a heart attack in that it is a high-probability, high-impact event that people seem to be ignoring. It is such a high-probability event that it is already happening, and that is the worldwide swing to the political Left.

I am not just talking here about what has happened in Bolivia, when energy industries were nationalized in that old-fashioned way by the new populist government of Evo Morales. But look at what has happened in Italy and in the United States with the midterm elections. Let me offer two explanations for this worldwide swing. One is inequality. It is terribly old-fashioned, and it is also staring us in the face. But many countries now have levels of inequality that have not been seen since the 1920s. In the United States, the top 0.01 percent of income earners now earn more than 2.5 percent of total income for the first time since before 1929. The ratio of a top executive's salary to an average worker's earnings was around 68 to 1 in 1940, and now it is closer to 200 to 1. This is not a peculiarly American phenomenon. It is what happens in globalization, particularly in countries lacking progressive tax systems. Rapid growth historically tends to generate returns at least initially to a relative minority of society in the absence of serious effort by the state to redistribute resources. And it is no profound or novel insight to say that such levels of inequality generate political backlashes.

The other cause, which might strike one as more paradoxical of the swing to the Left, is the increasing salience of immigration as an issue. One might think—probably rightly so—that the salience of immigration benefits the Right in most Western societies. But that is only half the story, because when immigration becomes a more salient issue, it tends to split the Right between moderate liberals reluctant to be seen as xenophobic and populists who do not mind being so seen. This is happening in so many countries that it would be tedious to list them. One example is the British National Party (BNP), which has made gains in local elections in Britain. Some polling suggests that 24 percent of British voters have considered voting BNP or are considering voting BNP, and as soon as adequate candidates are in place, there may be a dramatic shift to that party in Britain. And that will cost the Conservatives more votes than it will cost Labour; so this could be Gordon Brown's ticket to a long, long time in Downing Street.

My conclusion in brief is simply this: In 1914 investors, the best-informed people in the world, wholly failed to predict the outbreak of the First World War. Risk premiums did not start to rise until about July 22, 1914, at which point liquidity dried up so dramatically in the global system that all the world's stock markets, including New York's, had to close and stayed closed for the rest of that year, despite the obviously very high probability of a Great Power war in Europe in 1914. Why? Because contemporaries mistook liquidity for stability in financial markets. The extraordinary liquidity and low volatility of financial markets in the summer of 1914, which had been building since around 1900, created a false sense of security in the international bond market. And I think something very similar is happening today. Investors are failing to price in a global swing to the Left, even though it is staring them in the face and is historically entirely predictable. And that is because they are mistaking their own prosperity, as individuals and as a class, for everyone else's. So the bottom line is never mind the LPHIs; focus on the HPHIs, and we may just be all right.

Scott Barrett: I am interested in global discontinuities as the subject relates to the nexus between the international system and natural systems. My thesis is that the international system, consisting of 190 or so sovereign states, itself causes global discontinuities and thus needs to restructure itself to address these. I illustrate the problem with the example of global climate change.

There are two ways of thinking about climate change: gradual climate change, and abrupt climate change. Until the last few years the focus has been on the gradual, but the abrupt is much more interesting and should command our attention. A shift in the Gulf Stream, for example, would likely cause abrupt change that is not directly attributable to the effect of increasing concentrations of greenhouse gases in the atmosphere, but one that is triggered by them. Such a shift would cause a significant and abrupt change in the climate over, for example, northern Europe. How does the world as currently organized approach a problem like that?

All but a few of the world's countries have agreed that they want to avoid something called "dangerous interference in the climate system." That is very nice, but the problem is how to define and then identify the concentration level that is dangerous. Some have tried to do that. Greenhouse gases currently are at a level of concentration in the atmosphere of around 380 parts per million (ppm). Some think the dangerous threshold might be 400, others think it might be 450. The number most often mentioned is 550. Now the first problem is the absurdity of defining a point, say, 550 ppm, one side of which is considered safe and the other side of which is considered dangerous.

Another problem is that the international system consists of 190 or so nominally sovereign states, but the global climate system is unified. And there is a clash between these two worlds. The problem of climate change, like a lot of the other problems under the same kind of heading, has been caused by states acting independently. If a treaty system aims to meet a target of 550 ppm, say, how is individual responsibility for meeting that target assigned to each individual country and how can those countries be persuaded to accept that responsibility? The Kyoto Protocol is an attempt to do that, but I think it is going to fail because the program relies on enforcement that the current international system cannot deliver. Moving forward will demand substantial research and the development of new technologies that will change the nature of energy use worldwide. This cannot necessarily be a market-driven process. And the whole point about climate change is that it is a problem riddled with externalities. Governments must play a significant role. The approach taken so far is not going to be very helpful in that regard.

Furthermore, people will need to adapt to climate change, because it is going to happen. Adaptation means building resilience, in the sense that people and governments can withstand certain kinds of shocks, including climate shocks. Another intervention that is seldom mentioned is called geo-engineering. The climate is now being modified inadvertently; geo-engineering would deliberately alter the global climate. There are many different ideas about how this might be done. The most compelling method would deliberately put particles into the stratosphere that would reflect light and result in some cooling. It sounds like a fantastic idea, but it is already being done in a fashion. When power plants emit sulfur dioxide, for example, the aerosols sent into the atmosphere do cause some localized cooling. But the idea here is that geo-engineering would deliberately modify the climate on a larger scale.

Now, think about abrupt climate change. If, as will probably be the case, governments have not succeeded in mitigating the problem and are confronted with abrupt climate change, then this possible technology of geo-engineering will be important because it can cause a change in the climate much faster than mitigation can. It can be relatively inexpensive. It can be done as a big project rather than having to reduce the emissions of many different kinds of sources. However, it also introduces a new set of risks, such as ozone depletion.

Another problem is that global climate change would actually prove beneficial for some countries. Imagine a situation where abrupt climate change harms one set of countries but benefits another set. This geo-engineering technology—I am thinking more than fifty years ahead—can alter the climate. If countries that are harmed by abrupt climate change use this technology, the countries that benefit will inevitably feel the affects of that choice. How does the international system operate under this new kind of arrangement? Are countries entitled and allowed to make these choices independently? Or should they cooperate? They should cooperate, of course, but I remain fairly pessimistic about the ability of the current system to facilitate cooperation in order to address climate change.

Of course, the international system has not been entirely unsuccessful at cooperative efforts. One of its greatest achievements was the creation of a discontinuity—the eradication of smallpox. In the face of a pathogen that had killed millions of people worldwide, governments worked together to eradicate this disease. As far as is known, the virus still exists in just two places: in facilities in Atlanta, Georgia, and outside Moscow. There had been international discussion for years about destroying these remaining viruses, but in the wake of September 11 and subsequent anthrax attacks, the United States and Russia said they wanted to use the smallpox viruses in research to counter the threat of a bioterrorist use of the smallpox virus. By international agreement, the United States and Russia are carrying out research that is being monitored by the World Health Organization. This model could prove useful for dealing with climate change, where the world needs a system for regulating technologies with global impact but where it will not be in the collective interest to rely entirely on individual countries making decisions independently.

14

American Scenarios

A Discussion with
Walter Russell Mead, Eliot Cohen, Ruth Wedgwood, Anne Applebaum, Bernard-Henri Lévy, Josef Joffe, Peter Schwartz, and Francis Fukuyama

Walter Russell Mead: When I think about low-probability events, I find that the distinction between low- and not-so-low-probability events tends to blur. There are so many possible events, so many potential surprises, that it may be less important to think about the possibilities of given events occurring than to think about how to live in a world of growing uncertainty that is changing the tenor of life and politics even now. The future will witness dangerous, tragic, and threatening events—more low-probability events will occur, even if the probability that any one of them will occur does not change. The perception that the world is and will remain like this for a long time will have consequences long before many of these events occur.

What is perhaps most noteworthy about the coming into being of such a world is that we Westerners ourselves are bringing it about. Anglo-American capitalism is not a gradually improving Victorian garden party in which the service gets better and the food gradually gets nicer and fresher, but where nothing abrupt or rude happens. Rather, the more effective we are at doing what we do best—bringing more capital to more sensitive and flexible capital markets that reward more entrepreneurs and scientists, that lead to new technologies, new products, new industries, new ways of doing business—the more change in the world is accelerated.

This is not a new concept. Around 1915 Henry Adams looked at the history of the increase of human horsepower: the amount of muscle-power, then measured in horsepower, that human civilization could harness. He derived a parabolic curve going back to the Roman Empire that showed very slow growth at first and then started to steepen as machines came into the nineteenth century. He projected from the machine age into the electric age, and from that he predicted an ethereal age to start in the early decades of this century, precisely around the time Ray Kurzweil and others think the Singularity will come—an acceleration of technological change across the board so acute as to burst the bounds of human control. Henry Adams predicting the Singularity almost a century ago may be just coincidence. But the point that the pace of social, political, and technological change is accelerating is not coincidence—it is destiny. One can make an argument, call it a sort of cultural Malthusianism, that while the rate of change may be geometric or even logarithmic, the ability of societies to cope with change barely lifts off the linear.

Societies do gradually get better at mastering change, and some are better at it than others; nineteenth-century China was overwhelmed by the kinds of adaptations it needed to make while nineteenth-century Japan was not. Today, China is doing much better, although for how long no one knows. Social history suggests that as the pace of change increases, many societies around the world will be unable to keep up. That could happen in the United States, too.

When the gap between needed adaptations and actual adaptations gets large enough, there is a potential for an explosion of some kind. This is perhaps what the Bolshevik Revolution represented. Things were happening too fast in Russia for its institutions and cultural values to cope with what was happening. That created a cultural vulnerability. Such vulnerabilities will become more common in coming decades. To some degree al-Qaeda is an example of what can happen when societies are confronted with unavoidable change and pressures that they are incapable of mastering. An irresistible force hitting an immovable object produces an explosion.

Now, this is not a simple phenomenon, and there is nothing mechanistic or deterministic about it; I am speaking only metaphorically. This metaphor does attract considerable historical data, however. When the Sioux were feeling overwhelmed by the progress of white settlement, they came up with the ghost dancing phenomenon: They believed that if they wore special shirts and did certain dances, they would be invulnerable to bullets. They danced and went to war, but they could not prevail. Today, while al-Qaeda is behaving in ways not so dissimilar from those who launched the Boxer Rebellion or the ghost dancing phenomenon, they are able to inflict much more damage on their enemies. And if we speculate on how technology is likely to develop through the twenty-first century, ever smaller groups with ever fewer financial and other ordinary resources may be able to cause ever more disruption and mayhem. This is a pretty daunting prospect.

Let us put this in some historical perspective. The worst thing that could have happened to New York City on September 11, 1901, would have been that the British fleet, the most powerful in the world, could have sailed in and started shelling the town, as it had done, by the way, some years earlier. And that might have done less damage in dollar terms and would probably have killed fewer people than what happened on September 11, 2001. Now ask yourself what would be the worst thing that could happen on September 11, 2101. Vernor Vinge, the science fiction writer, talks about how at some point in this century a person will be able to go to a Radio Shack to buy the parts to build a bomb that can blow up California. The obvious point is that the tremendous rate of technological progress will vastly expand the opportunities for the human race to do bad things as well as good. The dangers the world faces are the inseparable companions of the achievements that most people are straining every nerve to create, enhance, and further.

So societies will not escape the human condition, but will experience a lot more of it. The twenty-first century will be an era of multiple singularities. Not only will information technology take off and the speed of change become vertical, but many cultures may face changes that seem to them to be apocalyptic in nature: the end of everything that is meaningful, that is desirable, that makes life worth living; events that destroy their ability to understand who they are, that threaten the core of their identities. And then there is the possibility of nuclear proliferation and war and multiple, superempowered terrorists who could bring an "end to history" in a somewhat different sense. This will be an apocalyptic era, an era in which people feel that ultimate questions of good and evil, and of human survival itself, are on the table all the time. No one will be bored.

Eliot Cohen: As moderator of this panel, I will ask you to speak very briefly on the significance of the apocalypse for American foreign policy.

Ruth Wedgwood: Only if I'm allowed to talk about Revelations next.

Eliot Cohen: Oh, why not?

Ruth Wedgwood: So here is a revelation: When I was at Harvard as an economic history undergrad, David Landes used to tell us that late entrants in economic competitions might have technological advantages. If so, then accelerating change might make life harder for an old, established power like the United States. This is something that Americans are going to have to live with and watch out for in a great many industries.

Beyond that, there are three reasons why the world ahead may be an unhappy place for Americans. First there is the Malthusianism of international labor markets. The happy belief that with open trade one can simply solve things by tax and transfer at the end of the day, which is the typical neoclassical apology for uneven talent and creativity in the world, does not work with open capital accounts. Capital will flee if it is taxed too hard. So the fate of American labor has become a Malthusian one.

This cannot in any way be ameliorated by giving all American workers a master's degree, because Indians can also take master's degrees. So the only advantages one has is some form of location and social economics, for few things have to be done face-to-face. That is why immigration is such a big and controversial issue, because it effaces the last comparative advantage a locality has. Perhaps culture matters in the ability to innovate, and in the structure of the capital market. It is harder for two guys in a garage to get capital in India than it is for two similar guys in California. Then there is the issue of political stability. Peacekeeping is bad for American labor. If the political environment or the legal environment stabilizes in or around India or in Africa, then it becomes more tempting for American manufacturers to take their industry abroad, or to do call-forwarding abroad. Globalization means American workers will be competed down to the world price of labor. James Meade predicted this once upon a time in a funny little book, where he argued that with the net marginal productivity of labor with infinite supply at zero, the market price of labor approaches zero.

While immigration is about the reduction of distance, political life may involve the irrelevance of distance. I speak of cyber-nations. One does not really need territory any more. The assumption always was that territory was needed as a legal prerequisite to become a nation. But one can now outsource all the services that one needs to keep a common physical enterprise going. Indeed, one of the advantages of cyber-nations would be the end of some of the requirements for fights over territory. Secession would not have to be the knock-down, drag-out that it usually is. A state could have international personality and international voice without necessarily having an exclusive portfolio of territory. There have been divided states and microstates. Liechtenstein barely has 160 square kilometers. So we may see a process of separation between international voice and power and the artifact of territory. There have been some cyber-nations heretofore, including one put on the web by a

California entrepreneur that favors the umlaut and the letter *x*, the Republic of Lomar. But it is also an idea that has been put forward for resolving issues like Kashmir and even Jerusalem, where people can enjoy some of the accouterments of nationhood without sole claim to the territory involved.

That may be happy news, but my third point is an unhappy one: the death of deterrence. The fundamental premise of both U.S. national security and criminal law has been that deterrence works. But for certain worldviews, deterrence does not work. With deterritorialized actors, for example, deterrence does not readily work. So a fundamentally different era may be dawning, one in which an epistemological challenge is central—namely, that of defining, taking, and responding to hostile action. Issues like torture and privacy invasion, and other facets of civil liberties can and will be debated for a long time. But clearly the tasks that government will be asked and expected to do are very different from what they have been. Reactive government will no longer be satisfactory. Because deterrence no longer works, government needs to be an omniscient, panopticon, Benthamite government that can see the future. And that is a very hard thing for any government to do.

Anne Applebaum: I will not worry, for the moment, about the end of the world. Instead, I will posit the end of the "American world." Many assume that the United States will always be the dominant world power. But the day before World War I broke out, Europeans still thought that empires would always rule the world. They did not and could not know that they were standing on the edge of the abyss and that it was all about to end. We could well be in a similar position right now.

American power could decline sharply in many ways. Some are obvious. Iraq could turn out to be an even worse disaster than even the pessimists now expect. It could take more troops and more money; the United States could sink billions more dollars into Iraq's reconstruction, only to see it become a terrorist state in league with Iran.

Some of these ways are less obvious—one having to do with Russia. Policymakers and opinion leaders are staring so hard at the Middle East, and worrying so much about al-Qaeda, that other kinds of threats to American power may be missed. The relationships among the United States, Russia, western Europe, and China could shift significantly in the next two decades, producing a very different balance of world power. Consider that Russia controls most of the gas pipelines into western Europe and has recently shown that it intends to use this influence for political purposes. It has already done so in Ukraine, temporarily stopping the gas in a repricing negotiation. A deal between the Russian and German governments to build an undersea pipeline also appears to have political goals, namely, to enable Russia to sell gas to western Europe and still be able to cut off eastern Europe if it so chooses. When Russia cut off Ukraine the gas also started slowing down into Austria and Italy. What if Russia decided to use that power, every once in a while, when the Kremlin is upset about something—when it does not like being criticized about Chechnya, for example—and turns off the gas to western Europe. There will soon be politicians in western Europe who will say, in effect, "What do we get from the Americans that we really need nowadays? Nothing. Who needs the nuclear umbrella anymore? North Korea and Iran have nukes; so what? Only the Russians are important to us because they supply our gas."

At the same time, Russia is an increasingly wealthy country because of energy, no longer bothers even to claim that it is a democracy, and has been actively setting itself up as an alternative to the United States. So western Europe may slowly fall under Russian influence, as may eastern Europe for the same reason. Western Europe could pull away rapidly from the United States if energy prices are high enough and gas pressure comes fast enough. Russia is becoming friendlier with China, and while episodes of Russian-Chinese friendship tend not to last very long, the two countries could establish a temporary deal. China may then decide that, with Russia and western Europe neutralized, the People's Liberation Army can invade Taiwan. This is not hyperbole; we know that there are Chinese plans to invade Taiwan, and that it could happen at any moment.

This invasion would leave Japan, and southern and eastern Europe, in a terrible position: to befriend a neutralized western Europe that is dependent on Russia, or else to appeal to Russia itself. Latin America, which is heavily under the influence of the oil-enriched Venezuelan government, is also becoming actively antidemocratic and anti-American. Latin America might thus link up with the Russians and the Chinese. At the moment the Chinese are already searching Africa for sources of oil. A situation could then rapidly emerge in which a United States that does not produce and export oil becomes less and less influential in a world economy where countries are energy-dependent on Russia and China. This could spell the end of NATO. It could spell the end of American influence in Asia.

Think through the consequences of such a chain of events: Russia and China control the United Nations. The United States and liberal democratic values are no longer admired around the world. The Russian and Chinese systems, meanwhile, are no longer totalitarian in the traditional sense and even offer opportunity to international venture capitalists. Countries aspiring to improve their standard of living would then align themselves not with the United States, whose influence is waning, but with China, with whom they can trade more easily and more simply.

This is a little like what the world could very easily look like in a decade or so, particularly if the current situation undergoes a great shock—a global financial crash, or a regional nuclear war that the United States cannot manage to bring under control, for example. It is not the apocalypse, true. But it isn't pretty, either.

Eliot Cohen: OK, so we have apocalypse, panopticon government, and the collapse of American power. Bernard-Henri Lévy, can you cheer us up, or do you have an even more dismal possibility in mind for America's future?

Bernard-Henri Lévy: It is most difficult to cheer up after all that we have heard. Let me lead up to my main point by commenting on the three presentations so far, in reverse order.

I agree with Anne Applebaum that we are obsessed with the Middle East and must learn to shift our gaze. I agree that Russia and China could constitute a real problem if they become complementary or "matching" allies, one with enormous manufacturing capacities and the other with the energy to sustain those capacities. Already the impact of these two countries can be seen, even when they are not allies but merely have parallel interests in a particular situation, like Iran. Russia and China hold the key to the solution of the problem, at least insofar as achieving and sustaining meaningful sanctions on Iran.

But what is the real nature of the relationship between American democracy and countries such as China and Russia? American strength does not rely on military power alone, or on economic domination, either, since this domination no longer exists as it once did. Russia and China still have to invest their money in American banks and hedge funds, and they send their young elites mainly to American schools. America is creative and its institutions in the broadest sense are the soundest in the world. Russia and China, India and Europe, nearly everyone in the world, holds these social and economic institutions in awe and has confidence in them. They have confidence, in a sense then, in the confidence that the American people have in their own system. In other words, the source and the seed of American power today is self-confidence, the optimism of the American people, and the American system itself.

Ruth Wedgwood is right to see in the problem of terrorism the dawn of a dark new era, one that is characterized by the obsolescence of the old order of frontiers, borders, territories, and so on. This is clear: al-Qaeda wages a war without front lines, in which every person can become a front line. But the territorial state as such is not dead. There are limits to the development of virtual, deterritorialized entities. Al-Qaeda thrived once inside a territorial state, Afghanistan. It may do so again, and also thrive in Pakistan. That is the reason I was from the beginning opposed to the launching of the war in Iraq, because I feared it would be a great diversion from the real problem. There is today one state that is still a territorial base for terrorism: Pakistan. If one spends time in Karachi, as I did when I wrote my book about Daniel Pearl's murder, one discovers a terrorist state based around Karachi and Islamabad. Territory matters.

I fear to be not less apocalyptic than Walter Russell Mead because history shows that all the major events of the twentieth century were low-probability events. None of them was predictable, none could be deduced nor predicted from any so-called laws of history. None of the early twentieth-century literature about the labor movement of Europe, for example, predicted that communism would take hold in the Soviet Union in 1917. No one predicted the synthesis of nationalism and socialism that produced Nazism through the strange molecular movement of two atoms, the national one and the socialist one. Not a single text in Germany, or in Europe in general, predicted a real mass movement of this sort that brought cataclysm and horror on such a scale. Even the Shoah, the genocide of the Jews, could not be predicted despite so many clear and obvious antecedents. Of course anti-Semitism was present in Europe for centuries and was expressed in every possible hypothesis *except* extermination. The Christian living in the era of Christianity could not conceive of extermination because Jews were necessary to the eschatological economy of redemption. And neither the anti-Semitism of the Enlightenment, in which Jews were hated for being traditionalists, and the reactionary anti-Semitism evoked by the Enlightenment, in which Jews were hated for being both foreign and modern, imagined extermination, but rather absorption. The Shoah was inscribed nowhere.

Neither was the end of communism. Hélène Carrère d'Encausse and André Amalrik may have predicted the end of Sovietism, the end of the Soviet empire, but not the end of communism itself. Even in the 1980s no one really predicted it. I remember meeting with Vâclav Havel, the future president of Czechoslovakia, seven months before the Velvet Revolution. He was then out of jail, about to go back into jail. He was a "proscrit," a hunted man. He was not in his own mind on the edge of becoming president, yet in fact he was. I remember President François Mitterand of France in his last big state visit: He went to East Germany. He believed deeply that communism had such a body, such flesh, that it could not be erased from the earth. And remember: in these years all the governments of Europe made deals with the Soviet Union, traded with the Soviet Union, and resigned themselves to the existence and virtual eternity of the Soviet Union. President Valéry Giscard d'Estaing closed his door to some dissidents in the East, believing that Europe would be divided for centuries to come. Indeed, the fall of the Soviet Union still remains an enigmatic phenomenon.

My main point comes in echo to Walter Russell Mead, and it is, in short, that there are two conceptions of history from which to choose. One conception, which is *consolatrice*, which comforts us and leads us to quote Kojève, is the conception of history's having a sense, a meaning, a purpose. This is a conception of history that not only predicts, but which links all events with all others in crisp dialectical patterns. It is meaning-making in its essence—constructivist in the broadest, metaphorical, and projective sense of the term. I believe, however, that the lessons of the twentieth century oblige us to consider another, completely different conception of history. This conception has been built by the anti-Hegelian current of twentieth-century philosophy. Georges Bataille, for example, says the only problem with Hegelian philosophy is that any real historical event is absolutely impossible to explain, to link with other events, or to place within a larger dialectic movement. Dialectics, said Bataille, in *La Part Maudite* and other books, works perfectly except to account for real events.[1] With a real event, there is no longer a dialectic, but instead a spark of history that illuminates with its short but intense light the real stakes society must face. Philosophy cannot rescue us from the low-probability events of the future, for it cannot even account for those of the past.

Eliot Cohen: Ah, more wonderful news: Apocalypse, panopticon government, the collapse of American power, and now the pointlessness of historical and philosophical analysis to even begin to help us through all of this. We are all going to hell in a handbasket and at the same time we are too thick to perceive it or to do anything about it.

I have been thinking about Frank Fukuyama's introductory challenge, however, which was, in part, to realize that surprises happen on the upside as well as the downside. I confess that I am one of those who is prone to focus on the bad breaks rather than the good ones. Nevertheless, I believe that America looks really good twenty-five years from now, and some of these upside characteristics can already be seen.

Both Europe and the United States have a serious immigrant problem, for example, but not of the same sort. European immigrants are demonstrating and even sometimes rioting. American immigrants are demonstrating, too, but they are waving American flags because they want to be incorporated faster into the United States, which is demographically better off than any other great power in the world, including China, certainly Russia, and certainly western Europe. I can also imagine a world in which U.S.-Chinese relations are not nearly as perilous as some people think they will be. Many assume that the Middle East is just a complete disaster, and perhaps it is. I am not sure we really know that yet, however. We have been talking about very low-probability events: asteroids hitting the earth, some uncontrolled chain reaction that squashes the planet down to the size of a football field, or a football. Compared to that, it is perhaps worth thinking that Iraq might turn out to be sort of OK. A reasonable person should at least consider the possibility.

If that is the case, it seems to me that the critical question is this: If the United States remains well positioned twenty years from now, what should it do with its power? After the end of the cold war, the United States suddenly found itself in an unprecedented position of tremendous power and influence, but unlike in 1947–48, without any real idea of how to use that power and influence. The United States might find itself in a similar position twenty years from now, so it might be worth investing some thinking now about the positive, longer-range purposes of American power. Then we can go back to worrying about nuclear terrorists and smallpox epidemics and the collapse of American preeminence.

Josef Joffe: I think one can fruitfully debate these three presentations and our moderator's comments as well on every single point. But I will pick just one: I want to pick on Walter Mead—actually, I want to pick on Henry Adams.

That the world changes geometrically but that man's capacity to change moves only linearly is an old idea. But is it true? I was thinking about how the world has changed in the last one hundred and fifty years, and I came up with a list. Of all the technologies whose social effects preoccupy us today, almost all of them are a hundred or almost a hundred and fifty years old. The biggest leap came in 1866 when the transatlantic telegraph line was laid down. That suddenly accelerated the time it took to get a message from London to New York by about a factor of 10,000. But the telegraph, the telephone, the car, the steamship, the diesel ship—all of these inventions have been around for a long time. Things have become a little faster, but in the 1930s there was a train that darted from Berlin to Hamburg in two hours, and it is only recently that new trains have beaten the record of the old "Flying Hamburger." So strangely enough, once critical inventions are in place, technology tends to move at a pace that allows people to adapt to them. What is really new? The computer and fiberoptics and all the rest have diluted, but not destroyed, the classical borders of the nation state. Governments have not lost control of their borders or their identities as states, and I don't think they will.

One other irresistible comment: Anne Applebaum is right to warn about the consequences of the pipeline net that the Russians have cast across Europe. It is a serious matter. But go one step further. What are the pipelines doing for Russia? Energy may be mainly in the hands of bad states, but energy riches also ensure that these bad states remain essentially weak because they stop development, they stop the growth of a stakeholder middle class, they stop markets from proper development, and they give energy state dictators wonderful tools to keep their states in the retrograde positions in which they find themselves. Is that so bad?

Anne Applebaum: I think the Internet, which is the really big technological change of the past decade, is a totally transforming innovation. It is not just a faster train—it is something very, very different. It took me a long time to work that out myself, but I now see that it changes the way news is going to be made, it changes the way commerce works, it even changes the way communities exist. It is going to change everything, and it is already doing so.

I was also struck by Walter's postulate that the very technologies considered to be the most revolutionary and exciting are also the ones that carry the most dangers. I think that is right, and the technology that comes most readily to my mind in this regard is bioengineering. Someone could steal the smallpox virus from a lab, but that would be difficult. At the same time, there are already twenty thousand sophisticated laboratories in the world and within a decade, a single person will be able to synthesize an existing virus. In these same labs, five people with just $2 million will, within a decade, be able to create an enhanced pathogen, a virus that can infect people who have been immunized with conventional vaccines, and kill perhaps a billion of them. And with an additional $3 million, these same five people could build a lab from scratch using equipment they can buy on the Internet. Now, this is the kind of technology we do not want to stop because it has a good chance of curing cancer and AIDS and of allowing people with genetic diseases to live normal lives. But this technology is also extremely difficult to control. It is not like nuclear technology, which requires expensive and sizable infrastructures to manage. Biotechnology is done in thousands of small labs all over the world. This technology, it seems to me, is a critical factor in the human future, for good and for ill.

Walter Russell Mead: I think the argument for accelerating technology and social change is a strong one. True, the transatlantic cable was laid in the nineteenth century. But it is also true that on September 11, 2001, fewer than half of the people alive in the world at that time had ever made one phone call. When modernization began in Great Britain, a generation had time to get used to its spread. Then they had to get used to the railroad, and they did. Then the telegraph. Then heavy industry. Now what tends to happen is the whole thing lands at once: People whose grandparents knew nothing but a rice paddy culture through the centuries are suddenly going through a compressed version of three hundred years at once. The industrial revolution in Asia makes it a far more complex social phenomenon than it ever was in Europe. Given the rapidity with which technological and hence social change is engulfing hundreds of millions of people, compared to the very slow speed of acculturation to technology in the past, I think it is possible to argue strongly for acceleration. We do have to worry about trends. Some project that the Japanese will go extinct in 2712, that the last Japanese will be a woman, that she will be 147 years old, and that she will be running a $800 trillion surplus with the United States.

Peter Schwartz: I think the forces for optimism are far, far greater than those for pessimism. The record of the past fifty years is unequivocal in that respect, in terms of how many more people are living well, how many more have climbed out of poverty, and how many more have been climbing out of poverty in the past twenty years, particularly in China and India. Looking a few decades ahead around the world, one is likely to see another two or three billion people climb out of poverty. And part of the reason for that is the distribution of knowledge around the world.

We have now realized that the way to help make countries rich is to spread knowledge and support better government. Governments that are reasonably honest and reasonably competent work far better than those that are not. This seems an almost trivially honest observation, but it has not always been obvious, and this dynamic certainly has proved not to be trivial. China and India are better governed today than they were twenty-five years ago. They are not yet good governments, certainly not great governments, but they are better governments. Nearly everyone in the world has access to knowledge today, thanks to the Internet. All the world can access Wikipedia and find out the latest knowledge on any subject. As a result, knowledge is spreading around the world, driving the creation of new markets and industries even as old industries are reinvented. This dynamic is unstoppable and the combination of those two things is, in my view, going to leave the United States and the world vastly better off twenty-five years from now.

Eliot Cohen: I was with you, Peter, until you mentioned Wikipedia, because I looked myself up on it, and that put me with the apocalypse crowd. The point being, I guess, that all information is not created equal, and the Internet, like all technologies, can be used for bad purposes as well as good ones.

Francis Fukuyama: I have a much simpler question for either Walter or Bernard-Henri Lévy: What's going to happen to "red state" America—to Walter Mead's famous Jacksonians—in the coming years? People in their analogous socioeconomic situation in Europe tend to vote Socialist, but they do not in the United States. Is that going to persist, or will the global Left that Niall Ferguson spoke about sweep them up, too? Will America swing to the Left, and if so, what role will "red state" people play?

Walter Russell Mead: I think "red state" Americans are populists more than leftists. They may want to raise the margin of progressive tax rates, for example, but they remain nationalistic, and at least borderline apocalyptic in their thinking. One of the reasons I think in apocalyptic terms is that so many Americans still read books on the end of the world, the "Left Behind" books, of which there are now seventy million in hardcover. The greatest single hardcover selling book in the history of the United States is Rick Warren's *The Purpose Driven Life*, another evangelical book.[2] I think people are responding to an environment they take to be more economically and more existentially threatening, by turning, not necessarily in orthodox ways, to religious sources of meaning and consolation. The decline of religion in much of the world, particularly in Europe, is related to a confidence that Enlightenment attitudes and technological fixes are going to solve the problems for which people in the past looked for supernatural help. But what happens if one's problems are with the historical process, and the most frightening prospects are in fact offshoots of the Enlightenment? That is where the supernatural returns to history, so to speak, and history begins again. I therefore see Jacksonian "red state" America continuing more or less on its current course.

Eliot Cohen: Let me now put that same question to the other members of the panel and broaden it a bit. I think most observers agree that American society is in one of its phases of religious revival, and that there is a rise in fundamentalist or evangelical religious sentiment. Does that translate in any important way in how the United States acts in the world? Might it do so in ways that may lead to surprising, unusual, or discontinuous types of behavior?

Bernard-Henri Lévy: I am not sure that the word *revival* is the right one to describe what is happening in the new evangelical American churches and especially the nondenominational churches. Having visited some of these big churches, my sense is that much more than another revival is at play. Revival means bringing new life to old faith. What I have observed in these big churches is a new sort of faith that relies on a new definition of the divine, in effect on a new definition of God. I believe that America is in a stage today of real religious revolution that is far more significant than a revival.

The old religions, including and especially the religions of America, were based on the Judeo-Christian idea of transcendence. God was conceived of as being here and there, of occasionally speaking to man, and then of being strangely, mysteriously silent. The new religions that are growing now, even if they take the same labels as the old religions, are based on a completely different conception of the divine. The new conception of the divine is one in which God is always present and always speaking. This new God never shuts up. He provides a testimony to believers in the car with them as they drive, in the bed when they sleep, in the garden with them when they cut the lawn, at the hairdresser's, and so on. This banalization of the divine, this denaturing of the divine, this end of transcendence, is something completely new. It introduces a new element to the old synthesis—of which America was the proof and Tocqueville the herald—which was a mixture of religion and enlightenment, of belief and reason. Tocqueville said that America was the only country where religion, enlightenment, democracy, faith, and human freedom flowed together in one direction, not as in Europe, where religion pointed one way and reason another. Now in America is a new phenomenon, based on a new definition of the divine, which could break this old alliance of enlightenment and faith.

Ruth Wedgwood: I constantly see before me in the UN Human Rights Committee the extent to which certainly central Europeans and even west Europeans are nervous about nontraditional religions, not allowing Mormons or Scientologists or anything that's evangelical to function. They fear that religion has so potent a force that it could destabilize ordinary social mores and political arrangements. American pragmatism and the kaleidoscopic view we tend to take of religious diversity is much more hospitable to evangelical faith. The immediate knowledge of God that Bernard-Henri spoke of goes along very well with the instantaneous premise of the World Wide Web. If we can know everything else in the world right now and in real time, why would it be odd to suppose that we can know God that way, too? Besides, American Protestants have always believed in a historically active God. Abraham Lincoln and Robert

E. Lee certainly did. Woodrow Wilson, too. Manifest Destiny was rationalized in light of a historically active God. So the distance between old and new faith in America is perhaps not quite as great as Bernard-Henri suggests.

And there is more. If one lives in a very disassociated society, then communal worship becomes more attractive, and it hardly matters to many what is worshipped or exactly how. The quickening, exhilarating pace of their lives sustains for many the idea that they are somehow living in transcendental times, that this—whatever "this" is—cannot go on forever, that the world is approaching some kind of historical hinge point. And it may indeed be so. World history is not linear, after all; it is more of a punctuated equilibrium. It develops from catastrophe, recovers from catastrophe, and awaits the next catastrophe. History is really much more like a series of cultural and military asteroids hitting us, and what is most interesting about it all is how the recoveries proceed. This is not linearity, but neither is it Hegelian.

Anne Applebaum: My only comment on your question, Eliot, has to do with anti-Americanism. U.S. religiosity could, for example, in my negative scenario about the rapid decline of American power, become one of the factors that divides the United States from its traditional allies. The United States, this evangelical country, is obsessed with the Middle East and gets bogged down there. Meanwhile, post-religious Europe, never-religious China, and Russia, where God was stood up against the wall and shot along with many, many others, begin to perceive that they have more in common with each other than with a religious America.

Eliot Cohen: Let me then answer my own question. I used the word *revival,* but I could just as easily have used the word *awakening,* a more traditional American term going back to both the Great Awakening, and the Second Great Awakening in the 1830s and the 1840s. The religion of those awakenings was not traditional either. It was lay led, in effect antiecclesiastical, antihierarchy. It emphasized low church Protestant traits, particularly the centrality of the individual's unmediated relationship to God. It was Jeffersonian, and later perhaps Jacksonian in that sense, which is not in the least surprising since Jeffersonian and Jacksonian premises about society and politics arose from roughly two centuries of Protestant tradition. These awakenings generated religious forms and beliefs that would have seemed quite strange to an Anglican or a Catholic. The United States is in the middle of that now, making early twenty-first century America a profoundly religious country. One sees it in the American military, by the way. In the past those awakenings did not have much connection to American foreign policy, but now the world is different and there is much uncertainty about the broader impact of religion as a result.

Walter Russell Mead: One thing that many people fail to understand—many Europeans, in particular—about the rise of religion in American society and the Jacksonians is that historically American religion has been antiestablishment. Popular religion in America has been antiestablishment; the awakenings were waves of anti-elite feeling. That goes for the Jacksonian revivals, the Kentucky revivals of the early nineteenth century, and I think today's revival as well.

In terms of how all this now affects American foreign policy, I think that for some time the American foreign policy elite, like the American elite in general, has suffered a collapse of confidence. "Red state" Americans do not trust the liberal internationalist elite, and since the war in Iraq took an unpredicted turn, the neoconservative elite has suffered a similar fate. This is a problem because in foreign policy the sort of folk perception of global dynamics that people have does not necessarily provide a good, solid basis for strategy or policy. So Americans, as a society, are having trouble developing a serious conversation about foreign policy, and the collapse of confidence in elite judgment, partly on account of the rise of religious energies, is one major reason for it.

15

Afterword

Francis Fukuyama

The authors contributing to *Blindside* deal with the problem of anticipating and preparing for what at the time seem to be low-probability events but which in retrospect are often seen as inevitable. They do this from a number of perspectives. They address the methodology for confronting surprise on the part of organizations, governments, and individuals; they examine historical cases of surprise like the collapse of communism or the Asian financial crisis; and they look to possible sources of future surprises.

Across the chapters of this volume, it becomes clear that there are three fundamental reasons why we seem so often unprepared for the unexpected, even when the unexpected proves, as in the case of Hurricane Katrina, to have been anticipated by many. These reasons have to do with the nature of human cognition, poor or missing incentives to prepare, and a lack of institutions necessary to guard against surprising or catastrophic events.

By far the most complex set of problems centers on human cognitive failures to anticipate and prepare for the future. The chapter by Richard Posner and the one coauthored by Peter Schwartz and Doug Randall point out that many surprises should not be surprising at all: hurricanes, asteroid strikes, and political upheavals can be assigned probabilities that, when multiplied by their potential costs, should lead organizations and governments to take precautionary measures. The reasons why they do not are several. In the first place, political, corporate, and other leaders have a hard time properly discounting the present value of events that will take place in the future. Not only are these leaders cognitively not well disposed to making these calculations; the institutional roles they occupy discourage them from spending time worrying about a problem that will occur after they are out of office or their administration is replaced by one from another party.

One of the largest sources of cognitive failure has to do with shared mental models of how the world works that are often reinforced by the small-group dynamics of leadership or elite circles. David Hale points out that the Asian financial crisis blindsided the International Monetary Fund in part because its experience lay with sovereign governments, leading to a failure to foresee looming problems in private financial markets. Peter Schwartz's Global Business Network has built a business around forcing organizations to deliberately abandon their existing mental models. It takes a business and its discipline, because thinking outside of the box is something much easier said than done.

None of the chapters here discusses at length one glaring case of an elite group that locked itself into a mental model—the U.S. government's failure to anticipate and plan for an insurgency and civil war in Iraq following America's 2003 invasion of that country. That an ethnically divided posttotalitarian state should not make an easy transition to liberal democracy seems obvious to many people in hindsight. It is thus not surprising that a great deal of effort has been spent trying to understand why so many intelligent and experienced officials in the Bush administration could have gotten this wrong. The reason clearly has do to with shared and self-reinforcing models about how the world works: the belief in an untapped and universal thirst for democracy and freedom; disdain for regional experts who were never supporters of the invasion in the first place; and overinterpretation of other recent events, such as the 1991 Gulf War and the collapse of communism, that suggested relatively rapid and low-cost successes for American foreign policy.

The Waldrop and Landes chapters suggest other reasons for cognitive failure. While many did predict a Category Five hurricane hitting the Gulf Coast or a messy aftermath of invading Iraq, some future states of the world are hard if not impossible to predict because they emerge out of parallel developments whose interactions are not foreseeable. This is true not just of technologies of the past like electricity and the internal combustion automobile, but also of more contemporary ones like the microcomputer or the Internet. All the more reason to be wary of the crowd of high-tech seers and gurus who confidently predict the "next big thing," usually on the basis of straight-line guesses about extensions of existing trends. The way that future technologies will interact, both with each other and with their users, is an emergent property not predictable from precursor developments.

The second source of failure to prepare adequately for surprise events has to do with resources. Even if individuals or organizations are cognitively prepared for a future contingency, they often do not have the right incentives to hedge against it properly. Hedging is costly, and no organization can possibly hedge against all possible contingencies or future states of the world. Cost-benefit analysis, as Posner points out, can provide some guidance (assuming one has gotten the future probabilities close enough to right), but risks often spill across boundaries and jurisdictions in ways that leave them unhedged. Robert Lempert's chapter provides a sophisticated path toward modeling future states but one not every organization can take advantage of and prepare for.

Scott Barrett's chapter on new infectious diseases is a case in point regarding incentives. Governments may be motivated to make investments in public health if they are made aware that their own citizens are at risk. The problem with many diseases, however, is that they are pervaded by externalities. The outbreak of a new infectious disease in a poor Asian or African country will not affect just the health of its own citizens, but that of other countries to which the disease will spread. But the poor country does not have the resources to make the proper health investments on its own account, much less provide a spillover benefit to the rest of the world. And the rest of the world has much less incentive to spend money improving monitoring and health conditions in the poor country rather than within its own borders.

Imbalanced incentives also explain the American failure to deal with imminent energy security risks. As Gal Luft and Anne Korin explain, sugar cane ethanol is far more efficient than ethanol derived from corn, but protectionist pressures from American corn and sugar growers have produced subsidies for corn and tariffs protecting sugar that make no sense in energy policy terms. Here the problem is not cognitive but political: Incentives in the American political system are structured by interest groups and do not take larger public interests into account.

The final obstacle to properly guarding against risk is institutional. Hedging against future risks is not just costly; it also requires collective action, specifically, a sharing of decisionmaking authority and a pooling of resources across organizational and international boundaries. Many predictable risks, like global warming, threats to energy supplies, and infectious diseases constitute public bads, and their mitigation assumes the character of public goods, which economic theory says will be undersupplied by markets alone. Governments must step in to supply global public goods, but there is today a clear undersupply of international institutions in this regard.

When a good is public with relation to a single nation-state, then public authority can step in to provide it. Such was arguably the case, as William Bonvillian's chapter suggests, with the creation of the Defense Advanced Research Projects Agency, one of the more remarkable efforts at industrial policy. Things are more complicated at an international level. In the past, the United States as global hegemon unilaterally supplied certain global public goods like maritime security and support for an open international trading order, because it was in the U.S. interest to do so. (That large players will provide public goods unilaterally is a result predicted by Mancur Olson's theory of collective action.)[1] But American provision of these goods has been selective: While the United States has undertaken costly periodic interventions in the Persian Gulf to protect oil supplies, for example, it has felt no obligation to mitigate its own carbon emissions that affect everyone else in the world.

It is thus not clear that it is either desirable or possible for the United States to be, in Michael Mandelbaum's phrase, the world's government.[2] Existing international institutions like the United Nations and its specialized agencies (such as the World Health Organization and the World Food Program) have tried to fill the bill, but everyone senses that they will be unable to rise successfully to some of the catastrophic events that can be foreseen today.

This volume is only a beginning point for thinking about the questions of foresight and preparation for unexpected events. The debate between James Kurth and Gregg Easterbrook, as well as the panel discussion among members of *The American Interest*'s editorial board, provide some concrete projections of future trends and areas where we may be blindsided. But it is important to recognize the larger cognitive, political, and institutional frameworks within which leaders think about and plan for the future. We can predict with certainty that we will be surprised; we can and do anticipate an array of catastrophic future events. Unfortunately, the authors of this volume suggest that we can also predict with certainty that when they come, we will be inadequately prepared.

Notes

Chapter One

1. Richard A. Posner, *Catastrophe: Risk and Response* (Oxford University Press, 2004).

2. Gregg Easterbrook, *The Progress Paradox: How Life Gets Better While People Feel Worse* (New York: Random House, 2003).

Chapter Two

1. Alan W. Harris, "Chicken Little Was Right! The Risk from an Asteroid or Comet Impact," *Phi Kappa Phi Forum* (Winter/Spring 2006): 32.

2. See, for example, Howard Kunreuther and Mark Pauly, "Neglecting Disaster: Why Don't People Insure against Large Losses?" *Journal of Risk and Uncertainty* 28, no. 5 (2004): 5–21; W. Kip Viscusi, "Economic and Psychological Aspects of Valuing Risk Reduction," in *Determining the Value of Non-Marketed Goods: Economic, Psychological, and Policy Relevant Aspects of Contingent Valuation Methods,* edited by R. J. Kopp, W. W. Pommerehne, and N. Schwarz (Boston: Kluwer Academic, 1997), p. 83; Gary H. McClelland, William D. Schulze, and Don L. Coursey, "Insurance for Low-Probability Hazards: A Bimodal Response to Unlikely Events," *Journal of Risk and Uncertainty* 7, no. 1 (1993): 95–116; and Paul Slovic and others, "Preference for Insuring against Probable Small Losses: Insurance Implications," *Journal of Risk and Insurance* 44, no. 2 (1977): 237–58.

3. For an excellent discussion, see Ronald J. Daniels, Donald F. Kettl, and Howard Kunreuther, eds., *On Risk and Disaster: Lessons from Hurricane Katrina* (University of

Pennsylvania Press, 2006). For a brief treatment, building on the analysis in Richard A. Posner, *Catastrophe: Risk and Response* (Oxford University Press, 2004), see Richard A. Posner, "Our Incompetent Government," *New Republic*, Nov. 14, 2005, p. 23.

4. Mark Schleifstein and John McQuaid, "Special Report: Washing Away," *Times-Picayune*, June 23–27, 2002.

5. Editorial, "Our Unprotected Region: You Might Think 55 Months Would Be Enough to Produce an Anti-Terrorism Plan. You Would Be Wrong," *Washington Post*, April 3, 2006, p. A18.

6. There is progress in that direction. One can now get a college degree in emergency management (see www.training.fema.gov/emiweb/edu/collegelist) and join a professional organization, the International Association of Emergency Managers (www.iaem.com/index.htm).

7. Sharon Ghamari-Tabrizi, "Lethal Fantasies: With Its Eye on the 'Universal Adversary,' Homeland Security Is Failing to Prepare for More Likely, Foreseeable Catastrophes," *Bulletin of the Atomic Scientists* (Jan.-Feb. 2006): 20. This is not to say that a smaller, explicitly FEMA-centric model for the department would not have worked, a model in which the obviously constant need for natural disaster response would have maintained the budget for the far less frequent need (one would expect) to respond to mass-casualty terrorist attacks. That, indeed, was the model first proposed for such a department, before 9/11, by the Hart-Rudman Commission, a federal commission chartered to review comprehensively national security requirements for the twenty-first century.

8. Risk Management Solutions, "RMS Combines Real-Time Reconnaissance with Risk Models to Estimate Katrina Losses," press release, Sept. 19, 2005 (www.rms.com/newspress/pr_091905_hukatrina_lossmethodology.asp).

9. Mark Schleifstein and John McQuaid, "The Big One," *Times-Picayune*, June 24, 2002, p. 1.

10. Ferenc L. Toth, "Climate Policy in Light of Climate Science: The ICLIPS Project," *Climatic Change* 56, nos. 1–2 (2003): 7–11. See also Thomas Bruckner and others, "Methodological Aspects of the Tolerable Windows Approach," *Climatic Change* 56, nos. 1–2 (2003): 73–89.

Chapter Four

1. See the study by Kirsten Lundberg for Ernest May and Philip Zelikow at the Kennedy School of Government, Harvard University, *The CIA and the Fall of the Soviet Empire: The Politics of "Getting It Right,"* Case Study C16-94-1251.0.

2. Gerald K. Haines and Robert E. Leggett, eds., *CIA's Analysis of the Soviet Union, 1947–91* (CIA, Center for the Study of Intelligence, 2001). For our results, see Bruce D. Berkowitz and Jeffrey T. Richelson, "Predicting Soviet Collapse," *National Interest* no. 41 (Fall 1995): 36–47.

3. Aside from George F. Kennan's famous essay, "The Sources of Soviet Conduct," *Foreign Affairs* (July 1947): 566–82, see Andrei Amalrik, *Will the Soviet Union Survive*

until 1984? (New York: Harper & Row, 1970); and the Bernard Levin column from a September 1977 edition of *The Times* (of London), reprinted in "One Who Got It Right," *National Interest* (Spring 1993): 64–5).

4. Directorate of Intelligence, Central Intelligence Agency, "Soviet Economic Problems and Prospect," declassified memorandum of July 1977, available in Haines and Leggett, *CIA's Analysis of the Soviet Union, 1947–91.*

5. Presidential Directive/NSC 18, "U.S. National Strategy" (The White House, August 24, 1977) (www.jimmycarterlibrary.org/documents/pddirectives/pd18.pdf).

6. National Security Decision Directive 32, "U.S. National Security Strategy" (The White House, May 20, 1982). A declassified copy is available at (www.fas.org/irp/offdocs/nsdd/nsdd-032.htm).

7. See Kiron K. Skinner, Annelise Anderson, and Martin Anderson, eds., *Reagan in His Own Hand: The Writings of Ronald Reagan That Reveal His Revolutionary Vision for America* (New York: Free Press, 2001), pp. 30-1; also see my review, "Ronald Reagan on Reaganism," *Orbis* (Summer 2001): 475–84.

8. National Intelligence Council, *Domestic Stress on the Soviet System*, declassified National Intelligence Estimate (Washington, November 18, 1985).

9. Directorate of Intelligence, CIA, "Rising Political Instability under Gorbachev: Understanding the Problem and Prospects for Resolution" (April 1989), memorandum available in Benjamin B. Fischer, ed., *At Cold War's End: US Intelligence on the Soviet Union and Eastern Europe, 1989–1991* (Central Intelligence Agency, 1999) (www.cia.gov/csi/books/19335/art-1.html).

10. Office of Soviet Analysis, "The Soviet Cauldron," declassified typescript intelligence memorandum (April 1991), in Fischer, *At Cold War's End.*

11. George Bush and Brent Scowcroft, *A World Transformed* (New York: Alfred A. Knopf, 1999), p. 519.

12. Robert M. Gates, *From the Shadows: The Ultimate Insider's Story of Five Presidents and How They Won the Cold War* (New York: Simon & Schuster, 1997), p. 521.

13. Stansfield Turner, "Intelligence for a New World Order," *Foreign Affairs* (Fall 1991): p. 162.

14. Daniel Patrick Moynihan, S 126, "Abolition of the Central Intelligence Agency Act of 1995," introduced in the U.S. Senate on January 4, 1995, 104th Congress, first session.

15. See Loch Johnston, "The Aspin-Brown Intelligence Inquiry: Behind the Closed Doors of a Blue Ribbon Commission," *Studies in Intelligence* vol. 4, no. 3 (2004) (www.cia.gov/csi/studies/vol48no3/article01.html).

16. Bush and Scowcroft, *A World Transformed,* pp. 521–22.

17. National Security Directive 23, "United States Relations with the Soviet Union" (September 22, 1989) (bushlibrary.tamu.edu/research/directives.html).

18. Address to Members of the British Parliament (June 8, 1982) (www.reagan.utexas.edu/archives/speeches/1982/60882a.htm).

19. House Subcommittee on Evaluation, Permanent Select Committee on Intelligence, *Iran: Evaluation of U.S. Intelligence Performance prior to November 1978* (Government Printing Office, 1979).

20. "Key Judgments from October 2002 National Intelligence Estimate," *Iraq's Continuing Programs for Weapons of Mass Destruction*, presented at background briefing by a senior administration official, released by the White House (July 18, 2003).

Chapter Five

1. Paul Krugman, "The Myth of Asia's Miracle," *Foreign Affairs* (November/December, 1994).

2. Jim Walker, Credit Lyonnais Securities.

3. Simon Ogus and Danny Truell, "The Myth of Asian Growth" (London: SBC Warburg, June 1996).

4. UN report.

5. Graciela L. Kaminsky and Carmen M. Reinhart, "The Twin Crises: The Causes of Banking and Balance-of-Payments Problems," International Finance Discussion Papers 544 (Washington: Federal Reserve System, March 1996).

Chapter Six

1. Carlotta Perez, *Technological Revolutions and Financial Capital* (Cheltenham, U.K.: Edward Elgar, 2002). See also Robert D. Atkinson, *The Past and Future of America's Economy—Long Waves of Innovation That Power Cycles of Growth* (Cheltenham, U.K.: Edward Elgar 2004).

2. Warren G. Bennis and Patricia Ward Biederman, *Organizing Genius* (New York: Basic Books 1997) (innovation requires "great groups"); Robert W. Rycroft and Don E. Kash, "Innovation Policy for Complex Technologies," *Issues in Science and Technology* (Fall 1999) (www.issues.org/16.1/rycroft.htm) (innovation requires "collaborative networks").

3. These and the following details are from the biography of Loomis by Jennet Conant, *Tuxedo Park* (New York: Simon and Schuster, 2002).

4. The norms of the Rad Lab's "great groups" are common to other innovations—both before and after—including the lightbulb at Edison's Menlo Park "Invention Factory," the transistor at Bell Labs, the integrated circuit and microchip efforts at Fairchild Semiconductor and Intel, the personal computer at Xerox PARC and Apple, and biotech advances at Genentech and Craig Venter's genomics projects. Venture capitalists typically try to find groups with similar characteristics. See, generally, Bennis and Biederman, *Organizing Genius*, pp. 196-218.

5. Vannevar Bush, "Science: The Endless Frontier" (Government Printing Office, 1945), pp. 1–11 (www.nsf.gov/od/lpa/nsf50/vbush1945.htm).

6. There are clearly major advantages to decentralized science. It creates a variety of pathways to scientific advance and a series of safety nets to ensure that multiple routes can be explored. Since scientific success is largely unpredictable, the "science czar" approach, of selecting early on a single science route, not a variety, risks major failures that a broad front of advance does not. Nonetheless, the United States largely lacks the

ability to coordinate its science efforts across agencies, particularly where advances that cut across disciplines require coordination and learning from networks. The solution is to sharply improve the ability to coordinate R&D across stovepipes without centralizing control. The current multiagency nanotechnology effort, the National Nanotechnology Initiative, marks one such attempt.

7. These details are from Licklider's biography by M. Mitchell Waldrop, *The Dream Machine* (New York: Viking, 2001).

8. J. C. R. Licklider, "Man-Computer Symbiosis," *IRE Transactions on Human Factors in Electronics* 1 (March 1960): 4–11.

9. DARPA, "Technology Transition" (1999) (www.darpa.mil/body/pdf/transition.pdf).

10. Description taken from DARPA, "DARPA—Bridging the Gap, Powered by Ideas" (February, 2005); DARPA, "DARPA over the Years" (October 27, 2003).

11. Marco Iansati and Roy Levien, *The Keystone Advantage* (Harvard Business School Press, 2005).

Chapter Seven

1. Milton Copulos, "America's Achilles Heel: The Hidden Cost of Imported Oil" (Washington: National Defense Council Foundation, 2003).

2. Testimony of Milton Copulos at a hearing on "The Hidden Cost of Oil," held by the Senate Foreign Relations Committee, March 30, 2006.

3. "Al Qaeda Warns of More Oil Plant Attacks," Reuters, February 26, 2006 (www.abc.net.au/news/newsitems/200602/s1578478.htm).

4. AFP, "Muslims Should Use Oil as a Weapon: Mahathir," October 4, 2002 (www.dailytimes.com.pk/default.asp?page=story_4-10-2002_pg4_3).

5. BBC, "Iran Wields Oil Embargo Threat," April 5, 2002.

6. "Exxon President Predicts Non-OPEC Peak in 10 Years," *Oil and Gas Journal*, December 13, 2004.

7. Selina Williams and Bhushan Bahree, "Energy Agency Sets Grim Oil Forecast," *Wall Street Journal*, November 8, 2005.

8. Testimony of Stuart Levey, Under Secretary, Office of Terrorism and Financial Intelligence, U.S. Department of the Treasury, before the Committee on Banking, Housing, and Urban Affairs, July 13, 2005.

9. Testimony of Secretary of State Condoleezza Rice, before the Senate Foreign Relations Committee, April 5, 2006.

10. Marianne Lavelle, "The Oil Rush," *U.S. News & World Report*, April 24, 2006.

11. Daniel Yergin, "Ensuring Energy Security," *Foreign Affairs* (March-April 2006).

12. Amory Lovins, *Winning the Oil Endgame* (Snowmass, Colo.: Rocky Mountain Institute, 2004).

13. David Luhnow and Geraldo Samor, "Bumper Crop," *Wall Street Journal*, January 9, 2006.

14. Worldwatch Institute, *State of the World 2006* (Washington: 2006), p. 74.

15. Dan Morgan, "Brazil's Biofuels Strategy Pays Off as Oil Prices Soar," *Washington Post*, June 18, 2005.

16. Johanna Mendelson-Forman and Norman A. Bailey, "Hooked-on-Oil Energy Substitute?" *Washington Times*, May 22, 2006.

17. George Olah, Alain Goeppert, and Surya Prakash, *Beyond Oil and Gas: The Methanol Economy* (Weinheim: Wiley, 2006).

Chapter Eight

1. David P. Fidler, "From International Sanitary Conventions to Global Health Security: The New International Health Regulations," *Chinese Journal of International Law* 4, no. 2 (2005): 325–92.

2. Mark S. Smolinski, Margaret A. Hamburg, and Joshua Lederberg, eds., *Microbial Threats to Health: Emergence, Detection, and Response* (Washington: National Academies Press, 2003), p. 8.

Chapter Nine

1. George Kennan, "The Sources of Soviet Conduct," *Foreign Affairs* (July 1947); the article was published under the pseudonym "X."

2. James Surowiecki, *The Wisdom of Crowds* (New York: Random House, 2004).

3. Robert William Fogel, *The Fourth Awakening and the Future of Egalitarianism* (University of Chicago Press, 2000). For examples of Bellah's writings, see *Beyond Belief: Essays on Religion in a Post-Traditional World,* 2nd ed. (University of California Press, 1991); *The Broken Covenant,* 2nd ed. (University of Chicago Press, 1992).

4. Peter Schwartz and Doug Randall, "An Abrupt Climate Change Scenario and Its Implications for United States National Security" (Emeryville, Calif.: Global Business Network, October 2003).

Chapter Ten

1. P. Wack, "The Gentle Art of Reperceiving—Scenarios: Shooting the Rapids" (part 2 of a two-part article). *Harvard Business Review* (November-December 1985): 2–14.

2. G. Treverton, *Reshaping National Intelligence for an Age of Information* (Cambridge University Press, 2001).

3. As quoted by Ronald Suskind, "Without a Doubt," *New York Times Magazine*, October 17, 2004.

4. P. F. Drucker, *The Age of Discontinuity* (New York: Harper and Row, 1968).

5. M. B. Ridgway, *Soldier: The Memoirs of Matthew B. Ridgway* (New York: Harper, 1956).

6. N. Nakicenovic, and others, *Special Report on Emissions Scenarios: A Special Report of Working Group III of the Intergovernmental Panel on Climate Change* (Cambridge University Press, 2000).

7. David G. Groves and Robert J. Lempert, "A New Analytic Method for Finding Policy-Relevant Scenarios," *Global Environmental Change* 17 (2007): 73–85.

8. R. J. Lempert, S. W. Popper, and S. C. Bankes, *Shaping the Next One Hundred Years: New Methods for Quantitative, Long-Term Policy Analysis*, (Santa Monica, Calif.: RAND, 2003).

Chapter Eleven

1. M. Mitchell Waldrop, *The Future of Computing* (Washington: Woodrow Wilson Center, 2004).

2. David Alan Grier, *When Computers Were Human* (Princeton University Press, 2005).

3. Vannevar Bush, "As We May Think," in *From Memex to Hypertext: Vannevar Bush and the Mind's Machine*, edited by James M. Nyce and Paul Kahn (San Diego: Academic Press, 1991), p. 89.

4. Larry Owens, "Vannevar Bush and the Differential Analyzer: The Text and Context of an Early Computer," in *From Memex to Hypertext*, edited by Nyce and Kahn, pp. 23–24.

5. Brian Randell, "The COLOSSUS," in *A History of Computing in the Twentieth Century*, edited by N. Metropolis, J. Howlett, and Gian-Carlo Rota (New York: Academic Press, 1980).

6. J. Presper Eckert Jr., "The ENIAC," *A History of Computing in the Twentieth Century*, edited by Metropolis, Howlett, and Rota, p. 525; and John W. Mauchly, "The ENIAC," *A History of Computing in the Twentieth Century*, edited by Metropolis, Howlett, and Rota, p. 541.

7. William Aspray, *John von Neumann and the Origins of Modern Computing* (MIT Press, 1990); William Aspray, "John von Neumann's Contributions to Computing and Computer Science," *Annals of the History of Computing* 11, no. 3: 189–95 (1989).

8. Paul E. Ceruzzi, *A History of Modern Computing* (MIT Press, 1998), chap. 7; Martin Campbell-Kelly and William Aspray, *Computer: A History of the Information Machine* (New York: Basic Books, 1996), chap. 10.

9. Tim Berners-Lee, *Weaving the Web: The Original Design and Ultimate Destiny of the World Wide Web by Its Inventor* (San Francisco: Harper, 1999).

10. M. Mitchell Waldrop, *The Dream Machine: J. C. Licklider and the Revolution That Made Computing Personal* (New York: Viking, 2001), chap. 2.

11. It is not even very hard. The assertion *If A then B* turns out to be logically equivalent to *(Not A) or B*. So any circuit that can embody *not* and *or* can also embody *if-then*.

12. William Aspray, "The Scientific Conceptualization of Information: A Survey," *Annals of the History of Computing* 7 (1985): 117–40.

13. Robert R. Everett, "Whirlwind," in *A History of Computing in the Twentieth Century*, edited by Metropolis, Howlett, and Rota; Kent C. Redmond and Thomas M. Smith, *Project Whirlwind: The History of a Pioneer Computer* (Bedford, Mass.: Digital Press, 1980).

14. "The Project MAC Interviews," *IEEE Annals of the History of Computing* 14, no. 2 (1992); Robert M. Fano, "Project MAC," in *Encyclopedia of Computer Science and Technology,* vol. 12. (New York: Marcel Decker, 1979).

15. Jaime Parker Pearson, ed., *Digital at Work: Snapshots from the First Thirty-Five Years* (Burlington, Mass.: Digital Press, 1992), p. 143.

16. Katie Hafner and Matthew Lyon, *Where Wizards Stay Up Late: The Origins of the Internet* (New York: Simon and Schuster, 1996).

17. Vinton G. Cerf and Robert E. Kahn, "A Protocol for Packet Network Interconnection," *IEEE Transactions on Communications Technology* COM-22, no. 5 (1974): 627–41.

Chapter Twelve

1. Fritz Stern, *The Politics of Cultural Despair* (University of California Press, 1961).

2. Benjamin Friedman, *The Moral Consequences of Economic Growth* (New York: Alfred A. Knopf, 2005).

Chapter Thirteen

1. Arthur Schlesinger, *The Bitter Heritage* (Boston: Houghton Mifflin, 1967), p. 79.

2. This episode was recounted to Rabinovich by James Craig, former senior official of the British Foreign Office.

Chapter Fourteen

1. Georges Bataille, *La Part Maudite* (Paris: Éditions de Minuit, 1949).

2. Tim LaHaye and Jerry B. Jenkins, *Left Behind: A Novel of the Earth's Last Days* (Carol Stream, Ill.: Tyndale House, 1995); Rick Warren, *The Purpose Driven Life: What on Earth Am I Here For?* (Grand Rapids, Mich.: Zondervan Publishing, 2002).

Afterword

1. Mancur Olson, *The Logic of Collective Action. Public Goods and the Theory of Groups* (Harvard University Press, 1965).

2. Michael Mandelbaum, *The Case for Goliath: How America Acts as the World's Government in the Twenty-First Century* (New York: Public Affairs, 2006).

Contributors

Anne Applebaum is with the *Washington Post.*

Scott Barrett is with Johns Hopkins University.

Bruce Berkowitz is with the Hoover Institution at Stanford University.

William B. Bonvillian is with the Massachusetts Institute of Technology.

Eliot Cohen, formerly of the executive committee of *The American Interest,* is now counselor to Secretary of State Condoleezza Rice.

Gregg Easterbrook is with *The Atlantic.*

Niall Ferguson is with Harvard University.

Francis Fukuyama, chairman of the editorial board of *The American Interest,* is with Johns Hopkins University.

David Hale is with Hale Advisers.

Owen Harries is with the Centre for Independent Studies (Australia).

Josef Joffe is a member of the executive committee of *The American Interest* and editor of *Die Zeit.*

Anne Korin is with the Institute for the Analysis of Global Security.

James Kurth is with Swarthmore College.

David Landes is an emeritus professor of Harvard University.

Robert Lempert is with the RAND Corporation.

Bernard-Henri Lévy is an independent journalist and a member of the editorial board of *The American Interest.*

Gal Luft is with the Institute for the Analysis of Global Security.

Walter Russell Mead is with the Council on Foreign Relations.

Richard A. Posner is with the University of Chicago School of Law.

Itamar Rabinovich is with Tel Aviv University.

Doug Randall is a partner with the Monitor Group.

Peter Schwartz is chairman and cofounder of Global Business Network and a partner with the Monitor Group.

M. Mitchell Waldrop is an independent writer.

Ruth Wedgwood is with Johns Hopkins University.

Index